Decoding Traces of Frank Courtis

Heather Thoday

A catalogue record for this book is available from the National Library of Australia

Dedicated to:

Jack

Ned

Miranda

Sam

Contents

This story has never been told,
because in the secret world
we could not, and cannot,
share what we do all day,
even with family and loved ones.

Rachel Noble, former Director-General,
Australian Signals Directorate[1]

---

[1] Rachel Noble, former Director-General, Australian Signals Directorate in 'Preface', John Fahey, *The Factory: The Official History of the Australian Signals Directorate*, Vol 1, 2023, vii.

Preface

No one has ever told the story of my grandmother's youngest brother, Frank Alfred Courtis. As his eldest grand-niece I am intrigued by the mystery that reverberates from the photographs and artefacts. Family stories framed him as a serviceman who had no long-term relationships, no children, no fixed address. A man of absence was the narrative I was given as a child.

During my teenage years, I heard about 'Uncle Frank' from my mother and her sister. The family narrative held Frank's endeavours as unremarkable. He was labelled as a journalist who was prone to playing practical jokes, and a RAAF serviceman who occasionally went overseas and brought back gifts. On the other hand, my Aunt Nancy, the intended recipient of Frank's writing and papers as detailed in his 1979 will, seemed to have strong connections with Frank.[2] She actively, yet unsuccessfully, sought to keep in contact with him, despite her ill-health. Nancy died in January 1989, just nine months before Frank. Frank's estate was managed by the Public Trustee of New South Wales, and his photographs, cameras, papers, writing and other artefacts were dispersed.[3]

I sought to discover more about this enigmatic family member, Frank Alfred Courtis. I wanted to add colour and substance to his life narrative. As I gathered traces of Frank's life, and reflected on

---

[2] See 12 December 1979 will of Frank Courtis, witnessed in Gosford, NSW. (H F Thoday collection)

[3] *Government Gazette of the State of New South Wales*, no 14, 25 January 1990, 755.

my own position as a teacher, academic and writer, I considered how growing up in Adelaide in the early twentieth century, entering wartime service, and navigating post-war Australia, shaped his life. I reflected that Frank's story resonated with my academic background in history, literature and sociocultural understandings.

Since the birth of my own children and grandchildren, I have sought to gather more knowledge about my family's heritage, with the intention of providing a different perspective and grounding of my children's place in their world. My recent publication, *Courtis Lines in South Australia*, provides a familial context for this biography.[4] Gathering the knowledge to truthfully tell these stories within their sociocultural context is a subjective enterprise. My understanding of Frank's story, which unfolds within these pages, will be read and rewritten by you, the reader, within the framework of your own context.

In my view, the loss of Frank's papers and direct artefacts is such a poignant loss of traces of Frank. *Decoding Traces of Frank Courtis* signals my own intention to revitalise the stories that have never been previously told or have been submerged under the layers of time. This biography traces his eclectic interests across a multitude of domains, including his theatrical pursuits, journalism and the emergence of military intelligence during the 1940s. The reader is taken on many journeys across Australia, the Pacific region, the United States of America, Canada, Europe and Korea. This account includes previously unconsidered aspects of his identity, including his engagement with parliamentary electioneering, his involvement in mapping Australia while in the employment of the Shell company, and his frequent visits to South Australia. My plan has been to tell Frank's stories to personalise his place in the world. A significant touch point for me is to view how his life intersects with themes of identity and belonging in twentieth century Australia. My hope is that *Decoding Traces of Frank Courtis* provides evidence that sparks curiosity in those who seek to locate further traces.

---

[4] Heather Thoday, *Courtis Lines in South Australia*, Staurolite Books, Gawler, 2024.

Acknowledgements

Gathering and linking the elusive traces of Frank's life has enabled me to apply my research skills in diverse aspects of twentieth century Australian culture, defence and identity politics. My understandings about life in South Australia during Frank's lifetime, particularly from 1930 to 1980, military intelligence, journalism, the role of war correspondents and the myriad impacts of World War Two on Australia and the Pacific region, have been amplified.

I acknowledge the First Nations custodians of the lands, rivers, oceans and sky in what is now known as Australia and Torres Strait Islands. This land has been traversed by the subjects of this narrative, one they have done with a twentieth-century worldview which generally denied First Nations peoples' spiritual and cultural connections to the land, waterways and sky. The individuals in this narrative could not appreciate that this custodianship has a history of tens of thousands of years.

Through this process of research and writing, I have had the privilege of connecting with family members who had personal interactions with Frank. In particular, I appreciate Frank's nephew-in-law's willingness to meet and to engage in conversations about Frank, particularly with relevance to his life in the 1960s and 1970s. Just one of Frank's three nieces, my mother, Jenny, has been interviewed and provided further memories, many of them from her perspective as a child.

I am indebted to Craig Bensch, whose grandfather Trevor Bensch, was gifted one of Frank's ventriloquist figures, known as

'Archie' within Frank's family. The Bensch family are now fittingly the curators of this figure, ensuring that 'Archie' will undergo reconditioning at the Chicago workshop where the figure was created in 1948.

I am so pleased to have another opportunity to thank my Courtis relative, Joy Window, for generously offering her advice with grammar, proofreading and editing.

Credit is also extended to my publisher, Jeff Noble of Staurolite Books, particularly regarding his work using contemporary technology to invigorate the twentieth century images, as well as further editorial assistance.

Decoding Traces is only possible with the encouragement of those whom I immeasurably love. This has enabled me to persist and gather these traces and offer them for future research and understanding. I am forever grateful to Kim, Sam, Miranda, Olivia and Daniel.

Beginnings

races of the life of Frank Courtis reveal a man who pursued
unexpected pathways. An initial reading of his family indicates
the manual trades inherent in his Cornish ancestry. Frank's Courtis
family lines thread through South Australia and Western Australia,
following his grandparents' immigration from the Lizard Peninsula
in Cornwall.[5] Frank's father was an iron turner, his grandfather was
a ploughman and an agricultural labourer, and his grandmother's
family were shoemakers.[6] Further research has revealed the pursuit
of adventure that permeated Frank's lineage. Frank's parents
married and had their first child on the Kalgoorlie goldfields,
almost forty years after Frank's grandparents had sailed to South
Australia from Cornwall with their first child and fossicked on the
South Australian Barossa goldfields in the 1860s.[7] Frank's
unexpected tracks throughout his life trajectory are not without
historical precedents.

Frank Alfred Courtis was the fourth and youngest child born to
Alfred James Courtis and Emily Minnie Mary (nee Elliott) on 13
August 1914. At the time the family had just moved from living at
Schuetze Street, Mannum, South Australia, in a multi-generational
household, close to one or two of Alfred's brothers and their
families. Prior to Frank's birth, the small family had lived in Croydon

---

[5] Thoday, *Courtis Lines in South Australia*, op. cit., 1–4. Heather Thoday and Joy
Window, 'These shoes were made for walking', *The South Australian Genealogist*,
Vol 51, No 3, August 2024, 18.
[6] Birth Certificate of Jean Courtis, 27 June 1905, Boulder, Western Australia. (H F
Thoday collection); 'Atalanta' passenger list, April 1866, London and Plymouth to
Adelaide, theshipslists.com.
[7] Marriage Certificate of Alfred James Courtis and Emily Minnie Mary Elliott, 13
July 1904, Kalgoorlie, Western Australia. (H F Thoday collection)

for two or three years after moving from Mannum, and lived at Robert Street, West Croydon/Croydon Park (as the suburb was variously written on letters and envelopes).

Early childhood

Frank Alfred Courtis,c. 1917.
(H F Thoday collection)

Frank's eldest living siblings were Bessie, who was born in 1908, and Norman Elliott, who was born in 1912 in North Croydon. Frank was born just two-and-a-half years after the death of his eldest sister, Jean. Jean was born in 1905 in Kalgoorlie, Western Australia, then sadly died when just over five years old, and was buried in Mannum in January 1911. Poignantly, Frank lived with the photo of Jean above the family's mantelpiece in their sitting room in West Croydon/Croydon Park and later in their Elm Street,

Brighton home. Reminders of 'our little rose' echoed throughout the family's life.[8]

Frank's cheeky nature and assorted interests were evident from his pre-teens, as underscored through a story told by his older cousin, Mercy Lawrie (nee Payne). Frank and Norman shared a bedroom at Robert Street, West Croydon/Croydon Park. During their primary school years when their maternal grandmother (Celia Mary Elliott (nee Dodd)) lived with the family until her death in April 1931, the three of them were also sharing the bedroom with a pet spider in a cardboard box. Fortunately for Frank and Norman, according to family folklore, 'Grandma didn't mind'.[9]

Entrepreneurial spirit

Frank's lifelong creative and entrepreneurial spirit were evident when, according to Frank, in his late teens he tried to set up a grocery delivery business in West Croydon/Croydon Park during the early Depression years, perhaps between 1930 and 1932. However, he stated that the enterprise was unsuccessful because other Croydon grocers discerned the threat to their business and income.[10]

Beginning to experiment

Frank's ease with language and communication was expressed through his creative writing from his early years. He was presented with a book prize in April 1926 from the Mayor and Mayoress of Hindmarsh for an essay which he had written as an eleven-year-old student at Croydon Primary School. There no longer remains any evidence of the topic or content of the essay.[11]

On the other hand, in 1928, at fourteen years of age, Frank did not show much aptitude for drawing, and was again noted in one of

---

[8] Photograph of the Courtis family sitting-room and mantelpiece held in the Courtis family collection. (H F Thoday collection)
[9] Letter from Mercy Lawrie (nee Payne) to Jenny Evans (nee Dealy), 16 September 1991. (H F Thoday collection)
[10] 'From Coffs Harbor to Higgins', *The Bulletin*, Vol 89, no 4589, 17 February 1968, 20.
[11] *The Advertiser*, 27 May 1926, 13.

*Frank at rear left, about 1926, with his older siblings Bessie
and Norman, and his parents, Alfred James (Dick) and
Emily Minnie Mary (Min) Courtis. (H F Thoday collection)*

Adelaide's newspapers, *The Advertiser*: 'Object Drawing Grade I:
Pass: Frank A. Courtis.'[12]

On 19 October 1929, at fifteen years of age, Frank assisted at the
wedding of his only sister, Bessie, to Albert Dealy. There are no
photographs of this wedding in the family's local Baptist church at
Rosetta Street, West Croydon, nor at the reception held around the
corner at Frank's parents' home in Robert Street. This wedding was
celebrated within the austerity of the times, during the week that
the world shifted in economic terms, with the Wall Street Crash
signifying the beginning of the Great Depression. The minimal
traces of that wedding include the twenty-five-year-old garland,

---

[12.] 'School of Arts and Crafts. Examination Results.', *The Advertiser*, 21 December
1928, 20.

bow ties and embroidered jasmine that Frank and Bessie's parents, Min and Alfred, had worn at their Kalgoorlie wedding in 1904. These keepsakes had been preserved and were ornaments for use at the West Croydon wedding. Bessie's garland and Frank's white bow tie, alongside the bow ties of his brother Norman, and his new brother-in-law Albert, have continued to be preserved in the family's collection of artefacts.

Frank was a groomsman at his sister Bessie's wedding, 19 October 1929. No photographs remain. The garland, artificial flowers and bow ties have been preserved, having been previously worn for their parents' 1904 wedding on the Western Australian goldfields. (H F Thoday collection)

South Australian Railways

Frank continued to live with his parents and brother Norman, while attending The University of Adelaide and also Islington Technical College. He successfully passed subjects including English, Maths 1, Maths 2 and Physics, enabling him to become a Grade One, First Class, motor fitter with the South Australian Railways (SAR).[13] Throughout his career as a fitter, he continued his apprenticeship education, achieved prizes in 'motor fitting' and was commended at presentation events at the Adelaide Technical College. Frank was one of two Islington apprentices at his level who achieved the award of a coveted three-year scholarship as a machine technician: 'Scholarships Awarded by the S.A. Railways Commissioner, tenable for three years at the S.A. School of Mines and the Engineering Diploma Course – James H. Ralph. Frank A. Courtis.'[14, 15]

While employed by SAR as a motor fitter, a workplace accident resulted in his right and left fibulae being broken. His admission to the Royal Adelaide Hospital extended from 20 to

---

[13] 'Successful candidates in 1929 leaving examinations', *The Register News-Pictorial*, 9 January 1930, 17; 'Under six subjects', The Advertiser, 31 January 1930, 26.

[14] 'Apprentices to receive prizes tonight', *News*, 6 December 1933, 9.

[15] James (Jim) Hynam Ralph, sixteen years old, was on a 'country studentship' from Riverton High School in 1933, when both he and Frank achieved a three-year scholarship. Unlike Frank, Jim continued a trajectory of employment with the SAR and achievements in electrical engineering. He achieved with credits in electrical engineering at the School of Mines and Industries through to December 1936 and continued as a SAR employee until May 1947. He was an engineer throughout his working life. James was born at Riverton in 1917 and died at Findon in 1994. State Records of South Australia, 'Record of employment sheets - South Australian Railways' GRS 10638, Rail Commissioner, Series Date Range 1880-1976, Index Q-T, 29 September 2021, 4; Genealogy SA, 'James Ralph'.

Courtis father and sons, left to right, Norman Elliott, Alfred James, Frank Alfred, were all employed at SAR during the 1930s. This photograph depicts Norman, Alfred and Frank in front of unknown address; no date is noted. This photograph may have been taken just prior to Norman's wedding in 1935. (H F Thoday collection)

28 September in 1934, with the payment being covered by the SAR Hospital Fund.[16, 17]

Prior to his accident, during early 1934, Frank's physical prowess was evident when he participated in athletics events in geographically varied areas around Adelaide such as Hindmarsh, Walkerville and Belair, collecting prizes in short distance running and high jump.[18] Frank's brother, Norman, was also employed at Islington

---

[16.] Genealogy SA, 'Frank Courtis' 'Hospital, Asylum and Lying-in Admissions'.
[17.] See 'distinctive marks' noted on Recruitment Form Attestation No. 2434 'Frank Alfred Courtis', 'Royal Australian Air Force' 'Permanent Forces', Laverton, Victoria, 8 Oct 1936.
[18.] 'Athletics at Walkerville', *The Advertiser*, 2 April 1934, 9; 'Amateur sports at Belair', *News*, 24 April 1934, 9; 'Big crowd watches amateurs closely contested

Decoding Traces of Frank Courtis

Brothers—Frank is at the left of his older brother, Norman. Although there is no date, Frank's uniform and the photography studio name indicate that it may have been in 1936, the year of Frank's enlistment in the Citizens' Military Force and later in the RAAF. Photograph by Raeburn Studios, Adelaide. (H F Thoday collection)

and at least occasionally accompanied him in these pursuits. Norman included Frank as his best man when Norman and Gwenneth (Gwen) Ivy married at the Woodville Methodist Church in 1935.

Frank as groomsman, seated, at his brother's wedding. Gwen's sisters, Melba and Amy, were bridesmaids. Gwen's niece, Jean, was the flower girl. Male attendant alongside Norman is unknown. Photographer unknown, 1935. (H F Thoday collection)

Frank's success in diverse fields such as writing, mechanical technology and physical fitness contributed to his being an asset on his application to the Citizens Military Force in 1936 and also at his enlistment with the Royal Australian Air Force (RAAF) soon after his twenty-second birthday.

---

athletics', *The Advertiser*, 20 February 1936, 16.

Onwards and Upwards

Frank officially launched into his next career on 8 October 1936 when he enlisted with the RAAF. He began as an Aircraftman First Class (AC1) with the Recruit Training Squadron at Laverton, Victoria.

During Frank's service with the RAAF, he had two service numbers. Squadron Leader Frank Courtis's service record, held at the National Archives of Australia, indicates that he enlisted in 1936 with the Permanent Air Force (PMF), and then was appointed to a commission for the duration of the second World War in 1940 with the Commonwealth Air Force (CAF) or RAAF as it was referred to in Australia. The Record of Service form indicates that he was number 2434 from 1936 to November 1940. His Record of Service form as number 2102 was for the period from December 1940 until his medical discharge in October 1944.

After completing fourteen months of recruit training (from 8 October 1936 to 16 January 1938) at Laverton, followed by training at Point Cook from 17 January to 16 May 1938, Frank was posted to No. 2 Squadron at Laverton on 17 May 1938.

During 1936 and 1937 he completed a 'Signals Course' with a note on his form, 'Record of Service – Airmen (Permanent), RAAF' as 'Air Force No. 2434', indicating that he received a 'Pass: Special Distinction'.[19]

Frank's military record was annotated to show that he had recreation leave for Christmas 1938 and the early summer of 1939,

---

[19.] 'Record of Service – Airmen (Permanent)', 'Courtis, Frank Alfred: Service number 2102, Date of birth 13 August 1914, Place of birth Croydon SA, Place of enlistment Laverton, Next of kin, Courtis A', National Archives of Australia, Series number A8877, Item ID 15318553.

Aircraftman First Class AC1 Frank Alfred Courtis
at Laverton, Victoria, October 1936. (H F Thoday collection)

Decoding Traces of Frank Courtis

Aircraftman First Class AC1 Frank Alfred Courtis, probably on the same day that he was also photographed with his brother Norman, possibly in 1936. Note that this was not the uniform hat he was wearing at Laverton. Photograph by Raeburn Studios, Adelaide. (H F Thoday collection)

when he travelled with a RAAF aircraftman to Adelaide. Although the date of the photograph below is unknown, it was taken at a beach on the edge of suburban Adelaide, South Australia. The location may have been Grange, near Norman and Gwen's home, or near his parents' new home at Elm Street, Brighton, South Australia. This photograph is likely to have been taken in the late 1930s, since Frank was caught up in world-changing events that required him to be elsewhere from early 1939 onward, in the early stages of World War II.

From left, Alfred, Min, Gwen, Frank, an unnamed friend (may be a RAAF airman), Norman, no date, about December–January 1938–39. (H F Thoday collection)

This beach scene (about late 1938 to early 1939) depicted Frank and his unnamed friend with his parents, brother and sister-in-law in freer pre-war times, with pressing world issues bubbling on the horizon. Frank and his friend had obviously been swimming prior to the family unit gathering for a relaxed photograph. The identity of the photographer is lost. The loving bond among these family members proved strong during the decades ahead. This snapshot was captured prior to Frank's right lower leg injury, sustained in

February 1942 when he was aboard the MV *Derrymore*, torpedoed in the Java Sea at the fall of Singapore. A later photograph of Frank with his father, Alfred, and his brother-in-law, Albert, shows the double scarring on his right leg.

RAAF deployment to Darwin

Returning from leave, Frank was reassigned to No. 12 Squadron in February 1939. By the outbreak of World War II in September 1939, he was based in Darwin.

> *No. 12 Squadron was a ... [RAAF] ... general purpose, bomber and transport squadron. The squadron was formed in 1939 and saw combat in the South-West Pacific theatre of World War II. From 1941 to 1943, it mainly conducted maritime patrols off northern Australia.*[20]

No. 12 Squadron had begun to move to Darwin in July 1939 and became the first squadron to be based in the Northern Territory. The initial aircraft were stationed at Darwin's civil aerodrome and were placed so as to be strategically tasked to search for enemy vessels in Australian waters during 1939 and 1940. In preparation for the move from Victoria to northern Australia, during 1939, Frank satisfactorily completed the Air Gunnery Syllabus and the Wirraway Flight Maintenance Course with hours on an Anson and a Wirraway from both No. 2 Squadron and No. 12 Squadron. He trained alongside other personnel from No. 12 Squadron who were designated for Darwin.[21]

Government funding had been allocated in 1938 for the building of the first air base in Darwin. Laverton Airbase was altered significantly to temporarily accommodate the personnel, hangars and construction facilities, during the transition phase to build the new northern site. Canvas hangars, temporary canvas

---

[20] Fisher, Cec, 'An original member of 12 Squadron RAAF, his stories and photographic collection'. www.ozatwar.com/raaf/cecfisher.htm.
[21] Fisher, 'Laverton', ibid.

barracks, re-purposed wood trusses and, needless to say, canvas messes, dirt floors and ablution blocks were sited at Laverton. Cec Fisher, an armament fitter, who has written prolifically about No. 12 Squadron's experiences, recalls:

> *I am sure that all flying and maintenance personnel will remember, quite distinctly, that cold winter of 1939 in those draughty canvas hangars which became worse and worse as they continued to tear with the force of those icy southern winds, ... [while at the same time] ... tak[ing] up residency in canvas tents pending our move north.*[22]

During most of 1939, while infrastructure, from trestles and camp beds to armament and navigational equipment, was being constructed and adapted in preparation for defence needs in northern Australia, pilots and airmen (including Frank) were undertaking surveillance flights. These personnel included 'a new class of pilot' with skills as 'fitters and riggers' to act as 'second pilots'. Cec Fisher noted that all fitters and riggers were required to conduct maintenance checks and ensure safe transit during the long surveillance flights, and is quoted as remembering that this was a 'good idea'. Frank would have been ideally positioned for this role, given that he had achieved significant grades during his apprenticeship and during his four years as a mechanical fitter with the SAR. Fisher recalled 'the planned, long, coastal [surveillance] patrols from Darwin to Broome and return, and because of the slow speeds, the aircraft would often need a 40 hourly inspection'. Frank's military record was annotated to show that he trained on the flights from Laverton to Wilson's Promontory (where a signal station was set up in October 1939) while he was based at Laverton. Then, while with No. 12 Squadron in Darwin, he was most likely a 'part-time air gunner, wearing a brass "flying bullet" on the right sleeve ... [due to his capability to

---

[22.] Ibid.

be] proficient with radio, photography, gunnery, bombing and navigation'.[23]

On 1 July 1939, the first personnel were deployed to Darwin on the Burns Philp ship, SS *Marella*. The ship called in at the ports of Sydney where there was a transfer to SS *Montoro*, and on to Brisbane, then Thursday Island, before arriving at Darwin. Frank's military record implied that he may have been on board. Sweat soon saturated the men's uniforms, as they traded the icy winds of Laverton for the tropical heat of the north. Their temporary accommodation at Vestey's Meatworks, an enormous ex-abattoir which they nicknamed 'Bayview Mansions', tested their survival strategies and capabilities. Simultaneously, No. 12 Squadron scrambled to build a RAAF aerodrome and, remarkably, ensured coastal surveillance was a strong presence across the Kimberley region, northern Australia and in the Torres Strait.

'The wet season' as named by the non-Indigenous residents and newly arrived personnel—otherwise known as 'Balnba' and 'Dalay' rainy and monsoon seasons by the First Nations Larrakia peoples of the region—proved extraordinarily demanding for No. 12 Squadron.

'The difficulties of command and control of a squadron in such a remote location was causing RAAF HQ in Melbourne some headaches' was one of the prevalent euphemisms that described the complex logistics required to ensure the success of this enterprise. In contrast with personnel at all levels among the revellers, at both departure and arrival points where 'there was an intense round of social activities [such as those] around Melbourne, including some rather wild farewell parties', the achievement of a completed airbase and simultaneous surveillance was an astounding feat of human ingenuity.[24]

[23.] Ibid.

[24.] '12 Squadron History, RAAF': 'Deployment to Darwin', Australian military

The gruelling conditions of the northern Australian environment proved incredibly challenging for the personnel of No. 12 Squadron, particularly in relation to supplies. One example of the endurance and sheer determination was that, despite being accommodated in the non-operational Vestey's Meatworks, the Squadron maintained momentum, even when provided with sustenance such as cold, stewed, curried bully beef, sourced from tins stamped 1916. 'The wet season' as named by the non-Indigenous residents and newly arrived personnel—otherwise known as 'Balnba' and 'Dalay' rainy and monsoon seasons by the First Nations Larrakia peoples of the region—proved extraordinarily demanding for No. 12 Squadron. With

Frank (on the right) drinking from a coconut with a No. 12 Squadron colleague, on a Darwin foreshore, no date, probably around December 1939. (Image courtesy of Peter Dunn OAM, Australia at War)

aviation history, The Australian Military Aviation History Association, no date. https://raafdocumentary.com.

tinea, dermatitis and dengue fever being highly prevalent, as were the 'skinned knuckles, mashed fingers and sundry cuts among inexpert workmen', they surmounted these challenges and built more permanent waterproof accommodation.[25, 26] Frank and his RAAF colleagues were still able to enjoy beach breaks and sample local delights, such as drinking from coconuts, which were a relief from the monotony of hard physical work and the limited menu provided at the base.[27]

Traces of Frank's recreation during his deployment to Darwin air base can be found, including being part of a RAAF football team in November 1939.[28] A few weeks later, Frank's trademark creativity and performance technique provided a stand-out distraction for No. 12 Squadron's pre-Christmas 'gala concert' with music and comedy at the air base:

One of the offerings was a popular colloquial ventriloquist duo by Frank Courtice [sic] and his dummy, AC1 Jerry. As this 'took the mickey' out of the establishment it was well received. Despite rumours to the contrary, Frank was not penalised for this performance.[29]

Frank's commendable fitness levels continued to be on show during his years in the RAAF. His high jump skills were often

---

[25] 'Gulumoerrgin Larrakia seasons calendar'. The Country of Larrakia peoples is Darwin and the Darwin region. 'Balnba [November to December] is the season of the first rains … people say "big rain coming"'. 'Dalay [January to April] is the monsoon season.' No. 12 Squadron, including Frank, built the first airbase while they experienced Darwin's seasons for the first time, during the months of November through to April. https://nesplandscapes.edu.au/wp-content/uploads/2016/10/Gulumoerrgin-Larrakia-seasons-calendar.pdf.

[26] '12 Squadron History, RAAF': 'Deployment to Darwin', Australian military aviation history, The Australian Military Aviation History Association, no date. https:// raafdocumentary.com.

[27] Flight Sergeant Frank Courtis and Corporal Wetherall drinking from coconuts on a Darwin foreshore. Part of the photographic collection of No. 12 Squadron based in Darwin during WWII, compiled by Cec Fisher, op. cit. (Image courtesy of Peter Dunn OAM, Australia at War)

[28] 'Football', *Northern Standard*, 17 November 1939, 16.

[29] Cec Fisher, '12 Squadron History, RAAF': 'Operations in the tropics – 1939', Australian military aviation history, op. cit.

reported, such as at the RAAF sports event at Laverton in February 1937, where he achieved the enviable height of 'over 5 feet'.[30] His sporting involvement continued in Darwin, including at the 'annual inter-unit sports carnival' of October 1940, where he was noted as a champion high jumper.[31] Frank was an 'all rounder', also involved in other athletic and team sporting events from 1939 through to 1941 in the Northern Territory, Queensland and Victoria.[32]

Commission to Administrative and Special Duties Branch

Following one year during which minimal traces of Frank are evident on his RAAF record, on 20 December 1940 Frank was reassigned to Signals Headquarters at St Kilda Road, Melbourne. His highly diverse interests, physical fitness, flexibility, quick wit and

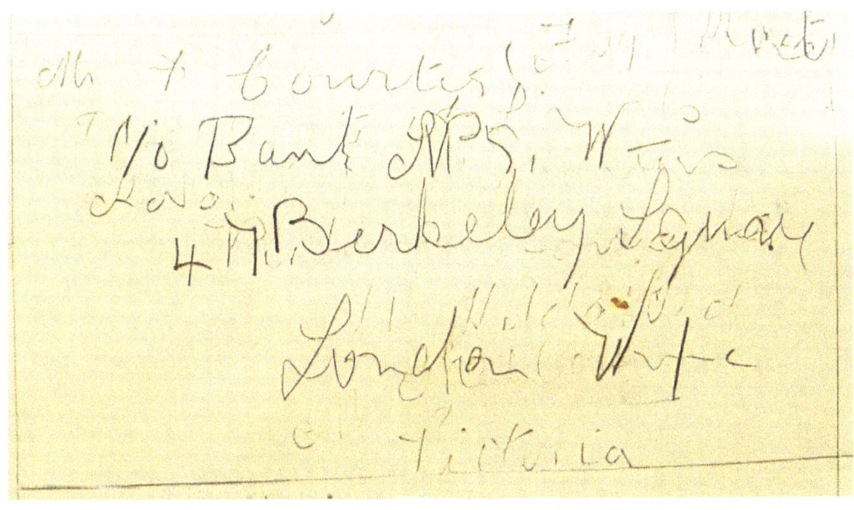

Excerpt from a page of Bessie Dealy's (nee Courtis) Bible containing addresses of family members, inscribed from the date of her marriage in 1929 until her death in 1957. (H F Thoday collection)

[30.] 'McCann takes all-round championship at R.A.A.F. sports', *Sun News-Pictorial*, 18 February 1937, 37.
[31.] 'Annual inter-unit sports carnival', *Northern Standard*, 4 October 1940, 9.
[32.] 'R.A.A.F. athletic meeting', *Northern Standard*, 16 April 1940, 1; 'Air staff beaten', *Air Force News*, 21 June 1941, 10.

strong language and communication skills may have led to his rapid promotion. As mentioned, he had completed courses in signals, air gunnery and Wirraway flight maintenance experience by 1940. The family Bible inscribed by Bessie, his sister (my grandmother), noted his address in 1940 as 'Directorate of Signals, RAAF Headquarters, Victoria Barracks, St Kilda Road, Melbourne, Victoria'. This address was written in pencil (perhaps in late 1940) and then partially erased before 1950 to show his later London address.

Frank's confidence and proliferation of writing in a more public forum became evident from 1940 onward. Concurrently, this was visible as he began his career in signals intelligence, which was also linked to international travel and journalism. To date, his first public published piece that I have discovered is 'Australia abroad', published in *The Bulletin* on 30 October 1940 and reproduced in the Appendix to this biography. Frank's poem has the same title as an article published on 25 January 1940 in the *Sydney Morning Herald,* with the poem being littered with apparent hints of references to the earlier newspaper article.[33,34]

> *Mr. Casey's appointment as [first] Minister to Washington is a notable development in our political history. It is the first full diplomatic appointment which this country has made, and as such it marks a break with the past … the recruitment of young men of the most promising type and their thorough training both in Australia and in the incomparable school of the British Foreign Office.*[35]

The newspaper article refers to the emerging capability of Australia's government to train and appoint professional personnel for leadership and staffing of Australian legations in Washington, Ottawa, Tokyo and elsewhere, in a changing world.

[33.] 'Australia abroad', *The Bulletin*, 30 October 1940, 35.
[34.] 'Australia abroad', *Sydney Morning Herald*, 25 January 1940, 10.
[35.] Ibid.

In December 1940, Frank was assigned to a commission with Administrative and Special Duties Branch.[36] From this point, Frank built on his early tasks of capturing and analysing signals and was positioned as an integral part of the interpretation of signals and strategic communication of this intelligence. This was a vital resource for those who were making decisions in conflict situations during and after World War II.

Frank's commission required him to work on communications within Central Bureau when it was initially located in St Kilda, Melbourne. Central Bureau was established as part of General Douglas MacArthur's Headquarters of the South-West Pacific Area from April 1942. Central Bureau later was relocated to Brisbane and known as Central Bureau Brisbane, a move which reflected Frank's location on his service record. Part of the role of staff at Central Bureau in Melbourne and, later, Central Bureau Brisbane was to obtain intelligence from Japanese-encoded communications by decoding signals. Australia worked across the three services— Air Force, Navy, Army—and with the United States, Canadian and British commands as appropriate.

Fall of Singapore

Throughout 1941, there are no verified traces of Frank until almost twelve months later, when he was posted as 'signals staff' on attachment to the Royal Air Force (British) at the RAF station at Kluang, Singapore. For this role, he embarked from Melbourne on 21 November 1941. This was presumably to work as a signals officer for the South-West Pacific Area Command, under General MacArthur's leadership.[37] Frank was certainly centrally placed during the Japanese bombings and movements to take Malaya and Singapore late in 1941 and early 1942.

[36.] See *Commonwealth of Australia Gazette*, No. 7, 16 January 1941, 105.
[37.] Fahey, op. cit., 69.

Decoding Traces of Frank Courtis

The first Japanese bombing of Singapore occurred on 8 December 1941, just two weeks after his posting to that location. The Japanese also bombed Malaya during late December 1941 and early January 1942. In December 1941 Japanese forces landed at Malaya and determinedly advanced southwards towards Singapore. Australians were among the Allied forces fighting to halt the advance. On 15 February 1942, the Japanese claimed victory, and more than 130,000 British and Allied troops were taken prisoner of war, including approximately 15,000 Australians.

To take a step back and look at the significance of events and their impact on Frank's work, it is vital to understand the wider context. With the outbreak of war in 1939, Singapore had become, in the minds of many Australians, a potent symbol of imperial strength and security. Such was its perceived importance that when Australia sent forces to bolster Singapore's defences (with Frank among them), many Australians felt that their men and women were defending their own nation.

The final defence of Singapore had cost Australia significantly.

The final defence of Singapore had cost Australia significantly. As well as thousands of prisoners of war, over 1,100 Australian troops were either confirmed dead or missing in action and hundreds of others remained unaccounted for, most having escaped shortly before or after the surrender. There was certainly scope for Frank in his cover role as journalist and particularly in his role as signals officer. His sister and their parents would have been highly vigilant at this time; that is, if they knew where he was positioned. As has become evident to many families in the years since World War II, communications between families and their loved ones on the front line were painfully slow or non-existent. Frank would have had delayed knowledge of the births of two of his nieces in 1941 and 1942. Likewise, Frank's sister Bessie and his immediate family would most likely have been unaware of his placement on the Pacific stage in February 1942.

Official evacuations of Allied personnel attempting to leave Singapore began in late January 1942 and continued up to the surrender of the Japanese. All RAAF squadrons were evacuated before the Japanese invasion, the last being No. 453 Squadron on 6 February. The last Royal Australian Navy warships had left by 12 February. Some work parties had stayed to destroy supplies and equipment and to repair a few remaining aircraft and vessels, but most of the armed services were evacuated by 12 February. A RAAF medical detachment remained on the island for another two days.

'Secret and confidential documents, files and publications likely to be of use to the enemy were destroyed by fire and other methods ...'

By then, the passage out of Singapore was extremely dangerous. However, Frank remained in Singapore, perhaps as part of the group who were destroying the last of signals equipment and signals records to ensure that these were unavailable to the Japanese. His recognisable writing style is evident in an article published on the front cover of *The Sun* following it being dispatched for publication in a Sydney newspaper by their 'Special Correspondent'.[38] The reporter recounted: 'Secret and confidential documents, files and publications likely to be of use to the enemy were destroyed by fire and other methods ...'[39]

At hot points during the war—such as just prior to the fall of Singapore—there were occasions when the ruthless destruction of primary sources, signals received and decoded and intelligence reports, was prolific, as referred to above. For military forces, this initially created difficulties for post-war intelligence development. A further ongoing impact has been that there remains little evidence for historians. Consequently, personnel such as Frank, were unable to speak of their past. Much of Frank's past has been shrouded in secrecy, despite documents recently

---

[38] 'A.I.F. & U.S. Forces in Java: Singapore holds Japs at bay', *The Sun*, 15 February 1942, 1.
[39] 'Adelaide airman's ordeal in the sea' *The Mail*, 18 April 1942, 7.

being made available for public perusal through the National Archives of Australia and the Australian War Memorial Archives.[40]

When Frank finally left Singapore on the cargo carrier MV *Derrymore,* the vessel was subsequently torpedoed on 13 February 1942. With MV *Derrymore* submerged below them, Frank was among 200 survivors who spent nineteen hours in the water among sharks and debris, before being rescued by the corvette HMAS *Ballarat.*[41] While awaiting rescue, Frank purportedly saved the life of John Grey Gorton. Fast forward, Frank later audaciously opposed John Gorton in the February 1968 Higgins by-election (see the section 'Federal by-election candidate'). John Gorton continued as the leader of the Liberal Party and the nineteenth Prime Minister of Australia from 10 January 1968 to 10 March 1971.

Frank recounted details of his injury in harrowing detail for Adelaide newspaper reporters:

> *On Friday the thirteenth we were well on the way, but that night a torpedo from a submarine blasted a hole in No. 4 hold, and our ship began to sink by the stern. My first reaction on landing back on deck after the explosion was to survey a gaping wound in my right shin ...*[42]

The article outlines Frank's account of how he was solely responsible for ensuring John Gorton was saved from drowning. However, there are no references to Frank's part in this episode in any contemporary publications that documented the life of John Gorton.[43]

---

[40] 'Record Search', 'Frank Courtis', National Archives of Australia; for more information about Korean War correspondents, see also Australian War Memorial Archives: https://www.awm.gov.au/articles/blog/war-correspondents-korea; https://www.awm.gov.au/visit/exhibitions/korea/faces/journalists. See also Major Hal Richardson, RL, includes details of Frank's confronting experiences as a war correspondent during the Korean War in 'War correspondent World War Two – Part 2', *Army*, May 1981, 10.

[41] Leslie W Hansen, 'MV Derrymore glass negative', 'Collections Online, Amgueddfa Cymru – Museum Wales', no date. https://museum.wales/collections/online/object/4d957b22-c1e1-33ff-a2b3-c01e71e3f07c/MV-Derrymore-glass-negative/.

[42] 'Adelaide airman's ordeal in the sea', op. cit.

[43] After his roles in the Royal Australian Air Force and serving as Australia's

The Mail reported that Frank convalesced at home and was eager to return to his assigned tasks in the Pacific War. His official record indicated that he required one month of medical leave.

A quarter of a century later, Frank reportedly told his audience of primarily Sydney readers in the *Australian Christian Record* of March 1968 that 'I think the Lord saved the Prime Minister'.[44] In my opinion, this is typical of Frank's play with words and use of irony, although a salt-water baptism may not have been appreciated by many readers. Having just been placed fourth in the unwinnable blue-ribbon seat in the 1968 Higgins by-election, Frank stated what he predicted the predominantly blue-ribbon readers would want to read.

Rewind to wartime. On 20 May 1942, Frank was reassigned as 'signals staff' with permanent status to 'Signals Defence' at Headquarters in Melbourne.

Relationships

At this point, it may be appropriate to comment a little more deeply on the influences that had been significant in the formation of Frank's character, personality, interests, spirituality, sexuality and understanding of his world in the twentieth century.

Throughout his life as a child and through to his mid-twenties, Frank's connections to the female members of his family have left traces that have been readily recoverable. Letters, cards, gifts, spoken memories and photographs indicate his deep care for the women in his life, including his mother Min, his sister Bessie and his nieces, Nancy, Jenny and Betty. It is evident from photographs and my conversations with those family members who knew him that he exuded an outgoing, intelligent and quirky character.

Prime Minister from 1968 to 1971, John Grey Gorton was knighted on Australia Day in 1977 by the Governor General, Sir John Kerr. A significant number of past conservative Prime Ministers have been nominated for and accepted this honour. 'John Gorton', Wikipedia, edited 20 September 2025.

44. 'Baptist man in shipwreck with Gorton', *Australian Church Record*, 21 March 1968, 6.

Opportunities to travel and experience a plethora of lifestyles, particularly during the late 1930s through to the 1950s, certainly opened opportunities for Frank to express his individuality and identity. Beyond the norms of an extended family household, he experienced shared accommodation under canvas and in military barracks, through the six Indigenous seasons of northern Australia, the icy cold of winter in Washington, Canada and Britain and the tropical climates of Manila, Singapore, Papua New Guinea and the Pacific. His friendships within the military forces were primarily with male colleagues where his flamboyance, sense of humour and eclectic interests were inherently encouraged and appreciated.[45] With Australian laws and early to mid-twentieth century social norms not necessarily reflected by his lifestyle, his early friendships with male colleagues either on base or on leave are exemplified by the photographs of him on the Darwin foreshore or at the Adelaide seaside.

Frank's friendships during World War II may have included the Central Bureau group in Brisbane, mentioned by two Australian historians of this era, David Dufty and John Fahey.[46] He may have at least been associated with the group of young men for whom hedonistic pursuits enabled them to enjoy life beyond the horrors of their military vocations, among whom Lieutenant-Colonel Alastair (known as Mick) Wallace Sandford was a key player. Simultaneously, Sandford was crucial in the initial planning and recommendations for the newly emerging cryptographic organisation

---

[45.] Frank's edgy sense of humour, channelled through the art of ventriloquism, was apparently risqué but within the confines of acceptability by the 'establishment', as noted by Cec Fisher, '12 Squadron History, RAAF': 'Operations in the tropics – 1939', *Australian military aviation history*, op. cit.

[46.] Dufty, op. cit., 145; Fahey, op. cit., 14.

which incorporated interception and analysis of coded military traffic, cryptography and intelligence reporting.[47] Sandford was '... an openly homosexual art-loving barrister and poet from one of South Australia's most prestigious business and political families.'[48] During 1942 to 1947:

> *... Sandford played the pivotal role in leading the Australian contingent at Central Bureau and successfully integrating it into both the British and American worldwide signals intelligence systems, [and] his sexuality was seen as criminal behaviour punishable by imprisonment ... Yet, despite his flamboyance and openness, Sandford successfully led Australia's military and diplomatic signals intelligence organisations, worked closely with his military superiors and enjoyed direct access to the heads of intelligence in both London and Washington and was widely regarded as an exceptional officer.[49]*

Frank's placement, according to his official military records, aligned closely with Sandford's postings to Queensland, Washington and London. On numerous occasions their paths crossed or their placement indicated that they were in close proximity. I would suggest that there was at least a sympathetic acquaintance, and that Frank had a high regard for Sandford. There are no solid traces that provide detail about Frank's friendships or relationships at this time. Australian law criminalised homosexuality and aligned with societal prejudices and thus ensured the discretion that would have been crucial during Frank's earlier life. It was not until the late 1960s and 1970s that wider social liberation protests, advocacy and decriminalisation brought about change in Australia. See the section, 'Dunstan decade' below for further understandings about Frank in the 1960s, revealed through the research for this

---

[47.] Fahey, ibid., 13.
[48.] Ibid.
[49.] Ibid., 14.

biography, and confirmed through several conversations with a family member.

New horizons in Washington and Ottawa

According to his official military records, by 15 November 1942, Frank was at Amberley RAAF Airbase, Ipswich, Queensland, awaiting a posting to Canada. This was deferred to 18 November 1942. Possibly he had been employed at St Kilda Road, Melbourne, in the early stages of awaiting these instructions regarding his future destination. He was placed with other defence force staff in Washington from 24 November 1942, as a RAAF representative to the Australian legation. The Australian legation to Washington was a fledgling structure, emerging with Australia's second minister, Sir Owen Dixon, in 1942. Broadly, the intention was to enable a united approach to sharing information and communication between Britain, the United States, Canada, New Zealand and Australia. In praxis, this proved to be an incredibly difficult exercise.[50]

Available traces show that Frank's role was most likely to have been essentially administrative, yet it was during 1943 that he was promoted to the rank of Squadron Leader. Primarily, he was responsible for the transcription and facilitation of communication between the Allies via cablegram. Examples are now open for viewing on the Australian Government Department of Foreign Affairs and Trade website. These 'most secret' 'historical documents' include 'cablegram 145' from Winston Churchill to John Curtin, dated 27 March 1943. This particular document detailed the strategies and reasoning behind numbers and types of United States' shore-based aircraft and RAAF forces in the South and South-West Pacific Areas.[51] 'Cablegram 152', dated 6 April 1943, from Owen Dixon to John Curtin is scribed on behalf of President

---

[50.] Bridge, Carl, 'Allies of a kind: Three wartime Australian ministers to the United States, 1940-46', in *Australia Goes to Washington: 75 Years of Australian Representation in the United States 1940-2015*, (eds) David Lowe, Carl Bridge, David Lee, ANU Press, Acton, 2016, 23.
[51.] 'Historical documents', '145 Churchill to Curtin', Cablegram Winch 6 London, 27 March 1943, 9.25 p.m., www.dfat.gov.au.

Franklin D Roosevelt, cordially conveying the impossibility of increasing the presence of either boots on the ground or aircraft, with the measured assumption that the current (1942) allocation of:

Australian and American forces … [should be enough] to preclude any serious attack on the continent of Australia.[52]

The National Archives of Australia holds minimal records reflecting the work of the Australian legation to Washington during 1942 and 1943. Frank's input is even less visible. One trace that is available for current viewing includes his signature to verify his perusal of revised office procedures on 2 July 1943.[53]

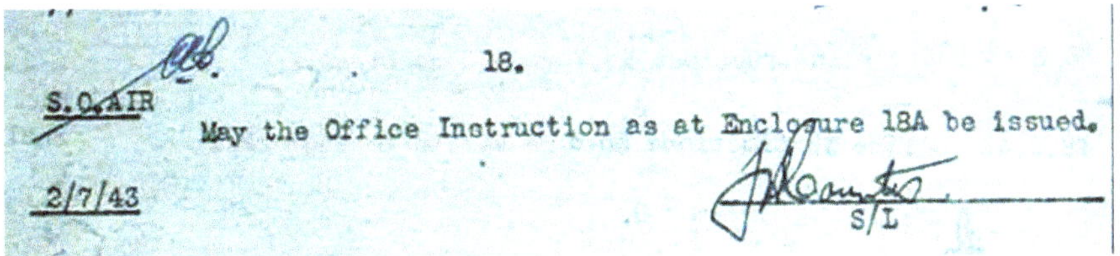

Verification of receipt of revised office instruction by Frank Courtis, Squadron Leader, 2 July 1943. (Image courtesy of National Archives of Australia. NAA: A1695, 6/306/ORG, 139382.)

While in Washington for his first Christmas, against the background of the world stage and impacts closer to Australia, Frank sent a traditional Christmas card to his sister Bessie and his nieces, Nancy and Jenny. However, his telegram also sent in 1943 suggests that he may have been travelling back and forth to assist with the emergence of the legation in Ottawa, capital city of Canada. A brief handwritten letter sent to his sister and nieces has been retained in the original envelope with the return address 'RAAF Representative, Munitions Building, War Department, Constitution Avenue, N.W., Washington 25, DC'. In the letter he noted: 'a whole year [has passed] since I came here. Doesn't time fly?'

---

[52] 'Historical documents', '152 Dixon to Curtin', Cablegram 571 Washington, 6 April 1943, 6.33 p.m., www.dfat.gov.au.
[53] 'Office procedure and instruction at RAAF representative Washington'. (Above image courtesy of National Archives of Australia. NAA: A1695, 6/306/ORG, 139382.)

His only brief reference to his work in November 1943 hinted at the differences among the camaraderie that he experienced while deployed:

Altogether, though, they [Americans] are very friendly towards Australians, who appear to be one of their favourite foreign nations—because we are 'foreigners' to them.[54]

In a personal aside in this letter he takes time to hint that he had purchased, and was bringing back to Australia after the war, at least one pair of fashionable 1940s silk stockings with back seams for his sister Bessie, playfully insisting that she no longer need to wear her Burson stockings.[55] (Burson stockings were widely available in Adelaide, advertised in the 1920s as fashionable yet comfortable for everyday wear. By the 1940s, Burson stockings had become the ugly, cheap alternative to the silk, back-seamed alternative, imported from North America.[56])

On completion of twelve months' service, primarily in Washington, Frank was posted to the newly formed Australian legation in Ottawa. In late 1943, the Ottawa post had been strategically structured to become an integral component of the international five-nations network known colloquially as the 'five eyes' military intelligence network.

Frank's telegraph to Bessie, despite being subjected to war-time scrutiny, let his family know that he would be in Ottawa for Christmas. This precious telegraph is glued inside of the back cover of the Courtis family Bible.

While Frank was attached to Washington in February 1943, the leader of Australian signals intelligence, Lieutenant Colonel Alastair Sandford, travelled to Washington and London, as part of the strategy to ensure the Australian element of

---

[54] Letter from Frank Courtis to (his nieces) Nancy Dealy and Jenny Dealy, November 1943.
[55] Interviews with Jenny Evans (nee Dealy), 1991–2025.
[56] 'Advertising', *The Age*, 7 December 1926, 7.

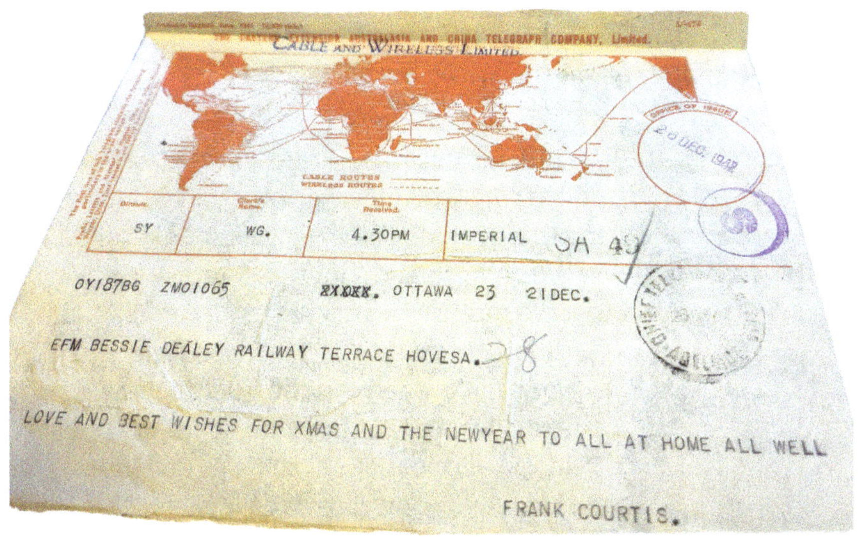

Frank Courtis sent this telegraph to his sister Bessie Dealy from Ottawa, 26 December 1942. (H F Thoday collection)

Defence, known as Central Bureau, was seen as Australia's national signals intelligence authority.[57] Americans and Canadians were dismissive of Australia's inclusion in military intelligence operations, but Sandford successfully smoothed relations and built connections. Indeed, historians unanimously agree that work under the leadership of Sandford at this time was pivotal to the formation of not only Central Bureau and Central Bureau Brisbane, but also to the formation of today's Australian Signals Directorate.[58] Evidence points to Frank as undoubtedly part of:

Central Bureau Brisbane [that] was initiated early in 1942, enabling Australians, Americans, Britons, Canadians and New Zealand personnel to work together to defeat Japan and then Germany. [John Fahey's] The Factory tells the story of how Australia's talented signals intelligence amateurs took an ad hoc wartime organisation and made it a national

---

[57.] Fahey, op. cit., 81.
[58.] Ibid., 473.

agency that became a highly regarded member of the 'five eyes' signals intelligence system.[59]

According to his official records, Frank left Ottawa on 4 February 1944, disembarking at Amberley nine days later on 13 February 1944. During this nine-day block, he must have landed en route, potentially in Washington, or in the South-West Pacific Area. Further unanswered questions arise, with an undocumented time between 4 March to 20 June 1944. He may have been in the South-West Pacific Area during this time and perhaps involved in an accident or subject to illness, as documentation provides evidence that he was on medical leave and hospitalised for one month immediately afterwards, from 20 June to 19 July 1944. Frank's presence at the Number 6 RAAF Hospital at Heidelberg, Victoria is noted in a Personnel Occurrence Report.[60] His record does not include the reason for his placement at the extremely busy hospital, which had recently been upgraded so as to accommodate four hundred patients. Frank was not subject to further impacts on his overall health, during the remainder of his life.

Frank had served almost exactly eight years of military service.

```
CORRIGENDA.

S/Ldr. F.A. COURTIS.        2102      Sigs.  Delete all reference to posting
                                             appearing in POR. No. 118/44.
                                             Officer now posted to 1 P.D., wef
                                             19/7.,   PZ 944.,   29/7.
```

Frank Alfred Courtis, service number 2102, was listed as a Squadron Leader with Signals at the time of his hospitalisation and declaration as medically unfit. (Image courtesy of National Archives of Australia. NAA: A1060k5, 30677383.)

---

[59] Ibid., dustcover.

[60] 'Corrigenda' is plural of 'corrigendum', a specialised word used in editing and publishing processes, meaning a mistake in a printed text that needs to be corrected. See Australian War Memorial Glossary for acronyms: PD: Personnel Depot; PZ: Pick-up zone; 'wef' indicates 'with effect from'; 'Volume 2 – Number 6 RAAF Hospital – Personnel Occurrence Report 1/1944 – 125/1944' 03 Jan 1944 – 11 Aug 1944. (Above image courtesy of National Archives of Australia. NAA: A1060k5, 30677383.)

His personal military record indicated that he was medically discharged from the Australian military forces on 19 July 1944 and declared permanently medically unfit three months later, on 4 October 1944. Frank had served almost exactly eight years of military service.

The character, Dorrigo Evans, in Richard Flanagan's novel, *The Narrow Road to the Deep North,* reminds me in some respects of Frank. Though Frank was not a prisoner of war like Evans, there are many touch points with Flanagan's narrative set in the South-West Pacific region. Frank seems to have doggedly pursued his own pathways following the closure of his official military service. Frank's decisions and post-war psyche, in the mid to late1940s, have affinity with those of Flanagan's fictional surgeon Evans. Flanagan writes about Evans:

The Japanese and the Germans may have surrendered in 1945, but ... [he]... hadn't and wouldn't for some time. He valiantly tried to keep his war going, lapping up any opportunities for adversity and intrigue and brinkmanship and adventure that presented themselves.[61]

War correspondent in Rabaul, New Britain

From October 1944, following his discharge from the RAAF for medical reasons, Frank was employed as a reporter for *The Age* in Melbourne. During this time, his electoral address was at Sherwood Street, Glen Iris, Victoria. Frank reconnected with the war in such a way that he became fully immersed in the South-West Pacific campaign. Notably, by August 1945, he was issued with a War Correspondent's Licence and Identification Card, as 'War Correspondent No.422' for the Commonwealth of Australia.

A pocket-sized blue trifold identification card was in the possession of his niece, Nancy (nee Dealy) Hodgetts, Frank's eldest niece, for about twenty years and has remained one of the artefacts

---

[61.] Richard Flanagan, *The Narrow Road to the Deep North*, 2013, 351.

Frank Courtis, Australian Military Forces War Correspondent No. 422 Licence and Identification Card. (H F THODAY collection)

in the family's collection. During the 1980s, Nancy had given it to her sister, Jenny (nee Dealy) Evans. This card reveals intriguing details of the parameters of his role as operational war correspondent with Group 5 in the South-West Pacific Area. Within six days of the card's issue, Frank was on a flight from Cairns to 'Moresby'.

This identification card links him to the official photograph of Frank Curtis (*sic*) alongside other war correspondents at Malaguna Mission, near Rabaul, New Britain, in the South-West Pacific Area during August through to late September 1945. The bay that is visible in this photograph is typical of the Gazelle Peninsula. The photograph was snapped during 'the first day of occupation of the Rabaul area by troops of 4 Infantry Brigade'.[62] The war correspondents reported on the process of the Japanese surrender at New Britain, their observations being dispatched to newspapers on the east coast of Australia and then copied to the newspapers of other Australian states and territories, before being published in international newspapers. Rabaul was a strategic location for Japanese forces in the Pacific, given the centrality of the town to islands and ports in the South-West Pacific, as well as close to the northern coastline of Australia.

Frank's dispatches from August to September 1945 were sent to two newspapers, *The Sydney Morning Herald* in Sydney and *The Age*

Frank Courtis is closest to the water, seated with war correspondents/journalists, Eric Thornton and Merv Warren, Malaguna Mission. Australian War Memorial/ Collection, Accession No. 096287. (Image courtesy of Australian Army History Unit, Department of Defence.)

---

[62] 'Malaguna Mission, New Britain, 1945-09-10. War correspondents typing their stories on the beach', Australian War Memorial/Collection, Accession Number 096287. (Image courtesy of Australian Army History Unit, Department of Defence.)

in Melbourne.[63] The information does not appear to have been directly copied into articles for publication, nor were there credits at that time to Frank as a war correspondent. Unlike his peers, Frank's war correspondence work was published anonymously in newspapers, as was common practice, or perhaps the information was used by another journalist. Unlike Frank's work, Eric Thornton's reports were credited with his name and published in South Australian and Queensland newspapers.[64] Merv Warren's writing was credited extensively in the *Brisbane Telegraph*, *Army News* and Western Australian newspapers.[65]

These sixty-five pages of dispatches, retained in the National Archives of Australia, point to Frank's experiences as an 'immersed' media representative and include some of his thoughts about humanity and the stark impacts of harsh warfare. Frank reported on the serendipitous readiness of the Japanese to surrender at Rabaul, a point that would not have been favourable for Australian newspaper readers. These lines in his dispatches are mostly erased, indicated by the words and phrases being struck through with red pencil. However, Frank's brief summative comments are completely spared the red pencil, such as 'The occupation thanks to the Japanese cooperation is proceeding to plan'.

Frank 'Courtis [was] on board *Glory* off Rabaul [on] six Sept' when:

> General Hitoshi Imamura signed surrender today ... At Imamura's request Vice Admiral Jin Ichi Kosaka C in C Jap

---

[63.] 'Press – war correspondents Frank Courtis – Despatches after the capture of Rabaul (Aug-Sep 1945)', National Archives of Australia, Location: Australian War Memorial, Series number AWM54, Control symbol 773/4/87, Item ID 473986. (Courtesy of Australian Army History Unit, Department of Defence.)

[64.] Eric Thornton, 'Australians at Rabaul: landing made yesterday', *The Advertiser*, September 1945, 1.

[65.] M C Warren, 'Australian occupation of Rabaul was one of biggest gambles', *Army News*, 3 October 1945, 3.

South Eastern Fleet also signed[,] using their own brushes and ink stop both signed with large Jap characters[.] Imamura added signature in English[.][66]

'The Instrument of Surrender' was signed on 6 September 1945, four days after the primary surrender document in Tokyo Bay on 2 September 1945. As reported by Frank and other war correspondents:

This … Second World War Instrument of Surrender by Japanese Forces in New Guinea, New Britain, New Ireland, Bougainville and adjacent islands … [was] signed by Lieutenant General Vernon Sturdee …, General Officer Commanding First Australian Army and Commander in Chief of the Japanese Imperial Southeastern Army, General Hitoshi Imamura … The signing took place on board the aircraft carrier HMS Glory *off the coast of Rabaul on the island of New Britain on 6 September 1945.*[67]

With the signing of the 6 September document, the liberation of prisoners of war began. Frank had access to them and was able to report on their situation in his dispatches.

The tension of imminent threat is threaded through Frank's dispatches, with the dispatch referring to the takeover of Japanese troops, hardware and claimed territory, communicated from Lae on 28 September 1945, indicating that:

Now the landing has been consolidated it can be revealed that this premature operation whereby a few hundred men

---

[66] Frank Courtis, 'Despatches after the capture of Rabaul', 7 September 1945. (Further dispatch references will continue to refer to dispatches by Frank Courtis.)
[67] Department of External Territories [1], Central Office, 'Instrument of Surrender – surrender of all Japanese Armed Forces in Papua New Guinea', signed on board HMS Glory, Rabaul Harbour, 6 September 1945. Held in National Archives of Australia. (Retrieved May 2025)

landed to contain and disarm eighty nine thousand Japanese had the makings of a massacre which could not have been countered had the enemy chosen to resist[.][68]

Frank's description of the raw and harrowing trauma of conflict depicted the brutalisation of prisoners of war, accounts of individual Japanese soldiers and a realistic assessment of the precarious, yet heroic, position of religious caregivers and health care services personnel.

These dispatches were richly informative of the lifestyles of disparate groups living at that time on the island of New Britain. The war correspondents had access to various community groups such as 'the Chinese internees' who had been captured and held by the Japanese as prisoners of war. The Chinese community was among those for whom the Instrument of Surrender signalled relief. Frank reported on the paradoxical 'sight of some of these [Chinese] children playing happily in puddles as their parents [lined up for the more serious task of being allocated rations] ... [in] a scene reminiscent of market day in a Chinese city'.[69] In a dispatch dated 12 September, he detailed the delight of Malayans at the available foods including fresh bananas and rice, revealed through their non-verbal language but also via the conversation in which he was able to utilise 'my halting Malayan learned during the campaign in Malaya'.[70] A contemporary reading of his dispatches might perceive that they are influenced by a degree of Allied propaganda, yet Frank appeared to maintain professional objectivity in a context of much despair, destruction and grief.

> **As an 'immersed' war correspondent ... Frank appeared to maintain professional objectivity in a context of much despair, destruction and grief.**

---

[68] Courtis, op. cit., dispatch, 28 September 1945.
[69] Ibid., dispatch, 23 September 1945.
[70] Ibid., dispatch, 12 September 1945.

Frank wrote in reverent detail, with examples littered throughout his dispatches, about the heroic and dangerous work of Anglican missionaries and Catholic priests and nuns, and particularly included respectful descriptions of the recovery and burial of remains of American and British soldiers, the curation of war graves and the retention of medals and rings worn by soldiers, before repatriation to the authorities of their respective countries. An example filled one entire dispatch, where Frank wrote of 'Rev Benson', an 'Anglican missionary', who 'lost touch with his party of eight men and two women missionaries' and was interred for three months in a 'Japanese camp' and then eight months in 'a military prison with Japanese criminals including murderers'.[71] Frank included the gruesome details of life within the prison camps, undoubtedly not suitable for newspaper republication in 1940s Australia, and therefore subjected to the dreaded red pencil. Frank's dispatch concluded:

> *Now he [Rev Benson] wishes to report to his bishop many things he felt he could not disclose to us as he told his story in the lamplight on a tent in the ANGAU [Australian New Guinea Administrative Unit] camp to which he was brought from Ramale Valley[.] Bearded and haggard at fifty eight but with his spirit intact he will carry on his work end message Courtis.[72]*

Interagency aid and cooperation featured significantly in Frank's dispatches, including some description of the Allied Intelligence Bureau (AIB) and the ANGAU, as demonstrated by Acting Major C G Roberts of ANGAU, who had been awarded the Military Cross for his

---

[71.] See also 'James Benson: Anglican missionary in New Guinea and Japanese Prisoner of War (POW)', *Pacific Wrecks*, 1995-–2025. Reverend James Benson returned to New Britain in 1946 and continued to assist with repatriation efforts. https://pacificwrecks.com/people/mission/benson/index.html.
[72.] Courtis, op. cit., dispatch, 21 September 1945.

work during World War I, and was the director of AIB.[73, 74, 75] At another point in the same dispatch, Frank mentioned the Red Cross Senior Representative, Richard George Scott of Tusmore, Adelaide, who was responsible for the provision of cigarettes, soap, chocolates, tinned fruit and 'reading matter'.[76] Simultaneously, Frank's dispatches were spared the red pencil when he reported candidly on the inadequacy of equipment and resources available for Australian and New Zealand troops.

Evocative portrayals occasionally splashed vivid scenes across Frank's dispatches, an example being his description of the ruined landscape of the township of Rabaul against the background of the four volcanoes of Simpson Harbour:

> *… the still water of Rabaul Harbour reflects the ever present clouds which seem to drop to the hilltops as though resting as evening approaches[.] But the scene is ugly[.] The bombing was intense and accurate[.] Ships have run ashore in a last desperate attempt to save their cargoes[.] Others have sunk at their anchorage with only funnels and masts showing above the surface of the water[.] Bomb craters have yielded to natures [sic] healing touch and their sides show a brilliant green of new growth which may be indicative of the future of this now desolate place[.] And pervading the atmosphere is the smell of death[.] Toiling the humid atmosphere up the nearby slopes at every step neatly hewn tunnels appeared where the Japanese had gone to earth to escape the terror*

[73.] 'Allied Intelligence Bureau', *Wikipedia*, last updated 23 July 2024. 'The Allied Intelligence Bureau (AIB) was a joint United States, Australian, Dutch, and British intelligence and special operations agency during World War Two. It was responsible for operating parties of spies and commandos behind Japanese lines in order to collect intelligence and conduct guerilla warfare against Japanese forces in the South-West Pacific.' AIB functioned between 1942 and 1946. Major C G Roberts is incorrectly reported as 'Major A A Roberts' by Frank Courtis, in his dispatch, 23 September 1945.
[74.] 'Caleb Grafton Roberts', *Wikipedia*, edited 10 November 2024.
[75.] 'Australian New Guinea Administrative Unit', *Wikipedia*, edited 18 January 2025.
[76.] Courtis, op. cit., dispatch, 21 September 1945.

from above as the allied counteroffensive mounted in intensity[.][77]

Frank reported in detail on the intricate Japanese infrastructure that became evident at this time:

Travel in the areas near Rabaul is like a page from the Arabian Nights [dash] except that there is no magic carpet [break] far from it [break] Footslogging over the steep mountains near Rabaul the Japanese tunnels constructed by slave labor [sic] reveal new wonders at almost each step [break] Entering these marvels of underground engineering one finds stacks of equipment and ammunition of all types running into millions of pounds proving beyond doubt that this base was intended for the invasion of Australia and New Zealand which fortunately never eventuated [break] End to end huge serial bombs torpedoes machine guns by the hundred field pieces of all sizes some mounted on efficient pneumatic carriages millions of rounds of small arms and field gun ammunition alternates with more scientific equipment [dash] complete radio stations photographic stores including aerial and cameras ...[78]

In contrast, Frank also reported candidly on human frailty and chaos, as he travelled on military vehicles near Rabaul. Most starkly, while surveying the inpatients of a field hospital, he recorded:

Today I saw human wreckage.[79]

On this and other occasions, he met and talked with patients, discussing their injuries and illnesses, using English, and other

---

[77.] Ibid., dispatch, 15 September 1945. My capitalisation at sentence beginnings, with my full stops at end of sentences.
[78.] Ibid., dispatch, 20 September 1945.
[79.] Ibid., dispatch, 15 September 1945.

languages with which he was equipped, including Pidgin, and his recently learned Malay vocabulary.

An eclectic mix of nationalities, professions and personalities were interwoven into Frank's dispatches, as he traversed the tracks, roads and regional areas around New Britain and New Guinea. One of his earliest dispatches recorded the wedding of Betty Millard of Glebe Point, Sydney, the first Australian Women's Army Service (AWAS) woman to be married in Lae, to RAAF Sergeant Glynn Hodges. Frank described the exquisite detail of the full length voile and taffeta dress, the clothing of the seven attendants and the tropical floral decorations.[80] The words of Frank's dispatch are echoed in an Australian newspaper article, 'First wedding at Lae', yet Frank's name is not evident.[81] This 'Lae wedding' was likewise reported Australia-wide by Frank's correspondent colleagues, such as Merv Warren, whose name was attached to his article.[82] In Frank's dispatches, other individuals were vividly described by Frank, including 'Timothy' or 'Mak Tim Keong', a young Chinese man, who had been an international student involved in football, swimming, rowing, boy scouts and school cadets, at Wesley College in Melbourne and spoke 'perfect English'.[83]

In one dispatch, Frank recalled that, unexpectedly, he had previously met up with two previous school acquaintances, RAAF Flight Lieutenant Doug Whyte and Sister Louise Godsen, on a Washington street in November 1943.[84] He also expressed his delight and surprise in meeting up with his Woodville High School alumni, David Moody, Royal Australian Navy (RAN), from Largs Bay, South Australia (during the 1920s, when both Frank and

> **Frank's dispatches were interwoven with an eclectic mix of nationalities, professions and personalities**

---

80. Ibid., dispatch, 29 August 1945.
81. Anonymous, 'First wedding at Lae', *Age*, 31 August 1945, 5.
82. Warren, M C, 'Full dress Lae wedding', *Daily News*, 30 August 1945, 3.
83. Courtis, dispatch, 21 September 1945.
84. Ibid., dispatch, 8 September 1945.

David attended Woodville High School). Frank reported that David, when nearing the time for his departure in September 1945 from Jacquinot Bay, southern New Britain, via a Navy vessel, stated '... quote it is grand to be at the end endquote'.[85] Interactions with diverse personalities such as these possibly give an insight into Frank's own multifaceted personality.

Multilayered traces

Traces of Frank also point to his posting during the mid-1940s as part of the Special Intelligence Section (SIS) following his discharge from the Royal Australian Air Force. Again, Frank's and Sandford's paths intersected at the time that Sandford was the lead officer of this SIS section from January 1943 to January 1944.[86] While Frank was later officially a journalist with *The Age* in Melbourne in late 1944 and early 1945, he was most likely simultaneously part of SIS. Earlier in the 1940s, when SIS moved to Brisbane and became known as Central Bureau Brisbane from 1942, Frank likewise moved to a Queensland address. Prior to 1939, 'Australia had no signals intelligence organisation, no human intelligence organisation and no intelligence capability whatsoever'. Yet as the nation's military intelligence proficiency grew, Frank was more than a casual observer of Australia's increasingly significant intelligence capabilities.[87]

The following year, a group of officers from Central Bureau Brisbane were photographed as they embarked from Archerfield Aerodrome, Queensland. They were travelling to Manila, Philippines, in 1945. According to Frank's military record, it seems likely that Frank was also posted to Manila at this time prior to his posting as

---

85. Ibid., dispatch, 7 September 1945.
86. Fahey, op. cit., 75.
87. Ibid., 203.

The group in the Archerfield Aerodrome included an unknown officer, Lieutenant-Colonel H (Roy) Booth; Colonel Alastair Wallace (Mick) Sandford, AIF, Deputy Director Central Bureau; Squadron Leader W (Bill) J Clarke, Bill, RAAF; Chief Signals Officer Central Bureau; and Lieutenant-Colonel Jack Ryan, Commanding Officer of the Australian Special Wireless Group. (Image courtesy of National Archives of Australia. NAA: P01443.045.)

war correspondent near Rabaul, New Britain, for six weeks from August to September 1945.[88]

During my research I discovered a volume of signals intelligence operations during World War Two.[89] It is available for viewing as a monograph through the Australian War Memorial.[90] I have also viewed it online, where it was listed for sale with Michael Treloar

---

[88] 'Brisbane, Qld, 1945-07, officers of the Central Bureau of intelligence at Archerfield Aerodrome', Australian War Memorial/Collection, Photograph, Accession number P01443.045.

[89] Dufty, David, *The Secret Code-Breakers of Central Bureau: How Australia's Signals-intelligence Network helped win the Pacific War*, 2017, 138. Dufty notes that United States signalmen in the Philippines collectively compiled a book, *Special Intelligence Service in the Far East*, named after the US component of Central Bureau, 'SIS Record Association' in 1946. Dufty noted that the author and publisher were a miscellaneous collection and were not identifiable. The book comprised photographs of Central Bureau locations and people and was captioned with light-hearted anecdotes.

[90] SIS Record Association, *Special intelligence service in the Far East, 1942-1946: an historical and pictorial record*, 1946.

Antiquarian Booksellers.[91] As I viewed the sample pages, one of the many photos showed signals staff formally posed in San Miguel, Philippines, I realised that Frank was among them. There was minimal textual information accompanying the photographs. However, it appears that Frank was also posted at this time to San Miguel in the Philippines. His presence in a photograph within the 'Signals Intelligence Service' book is unexpected. There is no explicit reference to this posting on his official papers held in the Australian National Archives. Part of the caption refers to 1945. The remainder of the caption states: 'Section of the Australian camp at the headquarters of the Central Bureau of Intelligence. This was the combined Australian Army, RAAF and US Army organisation whose function was to intercept and decode Japanese military signals.'[92] The accuracy of the date of this photograph is questionable, as Frank was discharged from the RAAF, on medical grounds, in October 1944.

Frank's involvement in signals intelligence was to have continuing reverberations throughout his life. 'In October 1945, [with] the war over ... [each of] Central Bureau; the Radio Security Service; the Special Intelligence Section; and their associated field units – was disbanded'.[93] However, Australian signals intelligence had established itself as a valuable component of national defence, as continued to be evident through Frank's activities for the remainder of the 1940s and through to the mid-1950s.

[91.] The monograph was listed with the author being 'George B. Frank (and numerous others)'. All other details correspond with those of the monograph accessible at the Australian War Memorial.
[92.] See also 'San Miguel, Philippines, 1945-06 [sic], section of the Australian Camp at the headquarters of the Central Bureau of intelligence', Australian War Memorial/Collection, Photograph, Accession number P01443.058.
[93.] Fahey, op. cit., 91.

Post-war Exploits

Frank's exploits in the six months immediately following the war are unclear due to lack of direct evidence. However, during late 1945 and through to 1946, it is now known that Central Bureau Brisbane was pulled back into the Directorate of Military Intelligence at Victoria Barracks in Melbourne, with Sandford continuing to head the organisation. Based on his previous roles during the war, Frank was likely to have been involved, as were a limited number of competent, highly secure personnel, in transferring the data and resources from Brisbane to Melbourne.[94] However, at this stage, I have been unable to ascertain whether Frank was involved alongside Sandford in the March 1946 meeting in London which led to the UKUSA agreement. This agreement informally enabled all 'five eyes' nations—Australia, Canada, New Zealand, the United Kingdom and the United States of America—to build their international cooperation with regard to military intelligence.

During the post-war years, Frank returned to Adelaide for short visits to his parents and sister Bessie and her family in Brighton, South Australia. He often arrived with gifts. Jenny has recalled that he brought a boat made of natural materials and a cutlery set made of mother of pearl from 'the islands'. He told his nieces that these gifts were from 'where he had been working'. Unknown to the girls these workplaces were at San Miguel, Philippines; Lae, New Guinea; and Rabaul, New Britain. Although Jenny was a young child at the time, Jenny remembers that the family fondly recalled

---

[94.] Ibid., 203.

Gift to his nieces, Nancy and Jenny, from Frank 1944–45. (H F Thoday collection)

and spoke about the occasions when Frank visited, including the occasion when he gifted the seamed silk stockings to his sister Bessie.[95]

By July 1946, Frank's feet were on Australian soil, ready to embark on a tour sponsored by the Shell petroleum company as part of their decade-long endeavour to complete their Around Australia Mapping Expedition. Albury's *Border Morning Mail* reported on Friday 26 July 1946 that 'places off the beaten track will be visited during a 10,000 miles' tour of outback NSW and Queensland in a utility van and specially equipped caravan trailer'.[96] In a similar vein, the fledgling 'The Australian Monthly Motor Manual' reported that post-war conditions were ideal for

---

[95.] Interviews with Jenny Evans, 1991–2025.
[96.] 'Untitled', *Border Morning Mail*, Albury NSW, 26 July 1946, 8; 'Shell Touring Service' *Cloncurry Advocate*, 13 July 1951, 4; '10,000 mile tour', unknown publisher, McCarron, Bird & Company, Printers, 479 Collins Street, Melbourne, no date, no page number.

touring. The article included an enlarged image of Frank, promoted tourism in Australia and highlighted that with 'more petrol … the touring season' was 'on'. An article, torn from an unidentified journal, has been in the possession of Bessie's family since 1946. The page included four photographs of Frank, 'a friend' and two Shell representatives. The 'friend' was dressed in military-style clothing and was mentioned and unnamed in the captions, as they prepared to embark on the tour.[97]

After completing this tour, according to a number of sources Frank may have begun freelancing as a journalist in Europe and the United Kingdom. Interestingly, his military intelligence colleague Sandford settled in Italy during this time and began employment as the manager of British Petroleum in Italy, with occasional return visits to South Australia, presumably to see his immediate family. Perhaps Frank was able to utilise his international contacts in Washington, Chicago, Ottawa, London and Europe as bases from which to build his career in freelance journalism.

Writing

During 1947, Frank continued to write and publish. His post-war writing reflected a genre that he occasionally adopted at other times of his life. He wrote as an anonymous author, created an atmosphere of fantasy and used word play with words of dual meaning, while also weaving in truth. One apparent product of this fantasy genre was the article 'Mid Shot (Half Shot) and Shell', published in August 1947.[98] This fantasy is narrated by 'The Wanderer', a reference to his later 1950s pseudonym as a journalist. 'The Wanderer' was an oft-used pseudonym in early twentieth-

Frank wrote as an anonymous author, created an atmosphere of fantasy and used word play with words of dual meaning, while also weaving in truth.

---

[97] 'More petrol and the touring season is on', *The Australian Monthly Motor Manual*, Vol. 1, No. 5, August 1946, 22.
[98] 'Mid Shot (Half Shot) and Shell', *Centralian Advocate*, 23 August 1947, 10, 11.

century newspaper narratives. Letters to newspaper editors in the 1940s posed as disclaimers, where writers point out that the use of a *nom de plum* had become too prevalent, and was at best a nonsense or, at worst, slanderous.[99]

The article 'Mid Shot (Half Shot) and Shell' told the fictional story of a shipwrecked couple who perilously negotiated the Timor Sea. The narrative is reminiscent of Frank's personal experience when floating in the seas of Singapore Strait following a torpedo attack on the MV *Derrymore* in February 1942. The author's reference to his childhood 'lithp' recalls Frank's own lisp, to which his sister referred during her own children's childhood. For Frank, this must have been a hurtful episode of short duration as a child, since it was no longer evident during his adult life. In this context, the reference provides Frank's signature to the narrative. Allusions to the layered meanings of 'shot' and 'shell' pepper the narrative, providing a multi-level effect for the reader to interpret.

Puppetry – Jerry and Archie

Late in 1948, Frank became the proud owner of a ventriloquist figure, created and manufactured by Frank Marshall. It was not Frank Courtis's first ventriloquist's puppet, as he had performed with 'Jerry, AC1' at the Darwin RAAF Base in 1939.[100] A handwritten inscription inside the head of the 1948 puppet (known as 'Archie', according to one of Frank's family), written at the time of manufacture, clearly points to its provenance:

> *MADE BY FRANK MARSHALL*
> *55115 LOOMIS 13480*
> *CHICAGO, M.E. USA*
> *MADE FOR*
> *CAPT. FRANK COURTIS*
> *27.7.48*

---

[99] 'Not "The Wanderer"', *Advocate*, 19 Sept 1945, 17.
[100] '12 Squadron History, RAAF', https:// raafdocumentary.com, op. cit.

'Archie' prior to reconditioning in 2025.
(H F Thoday collection)

The address in the puppet's head was Frank Marshall's home, where Frank Marshall had a workshop in 1948. The current company states that this puppet is not listed on their records. This figure appears to have been custom made for Frank Courtis. Although 'Archie' now has more modern clothing, the figure could have been shipped from the United States without clothing and with paper wrapping around the hands and face. The shoes are manufactured in the United States. At the time of publication, the current owner is pursuing the possibility of repairs and reconditioning by the contemporary manufacturers in Chicago, so that 'Archie' will again be completely functional.

> *Frank Marshall (born Frank Marzalkiewicz on March 9, 1900; died October 10, 1969) was a professional ventriloquist dummy, marionette and Punch and Judy maker who created many of the most famous ventriloquist dummies used during the United States's entertainment era through the Golden Age of Television. He is colloquially known as America's Geppetto.*[101]

It is likely that Frank's first ventriloquist figure, which he had named Jerry, was similar to a Frank Marshall production, as it had the same large eyes, bright red mouth and orange skin tones. This trace points to an intriguing aspect of Frank's personality. With Frank's constant movement around Australia and overseas, Jerry and Archie required storage at his parents' home in Brighton, South Australia. One of his nieces, who was a child at that time, has recalled that, during the late 1940s, Frank would entertain the family with one, and then later in the 1940s with both figures, during his visits to his parents' home. By the mid-1950s, he chose to 'gift forward' Jerry to a family member, and then a few years later, probably while preparing to sell his parents' home, he gifted Archie.[102]

---

[101] 'Frank Marshall (puppeteer)', *Wikipedia*, edited 20 June 2024.
[102] While Jerry's location is no longer known, Archie is currently in the custodianship of the descendants of Trevor Bensch.

The current owner of 'Archie', Craig Bensch, was gifted the figure by his grandfather, Trevor Bensch, in 2018.[103] Trevor was a Baptist minister at a number of Baptist churches from 1953 to 1984 and was later the chaplain at two South Australian hospitals, including the Queen Elizabeth Hospital. Trevor became a significant advocate in the voluntary assisted dying movement. He spoke in Parliament and was invited to speak across Australia. Trevor passed away in January 2019.

Craig's grandfather did not provide any details about how he received the puppet from Frank, although Craig believes Trevor was given the puppet in exchange for public speaking or preaching. Trevor Bensch began his ministry with the Baptist church at Port Lincoln for five years, from 1953.[104] This was followed by a ministry at Port Pirie South Baptist Church, commencing in 1956.[105] By Christmas 1959, Trevor had begun a short appointment as minister at Ramsbottom Baptist and Banklane Baptist Churches in England.[106] Although there is no documented occasion where both Trevor and Frank met, they would have been known to each other, particularly as they both moved in Baptist circles. Although Trevor was ten years younger than Frank, both men were contemporaries who preached and wrote about controversial topics such as Sunday church not being the singular place where Christianity could be experienced, and the exploration of spirituality through the art of public performance.

Freelance Journalist, War Correspondent in Korea

Frank was a freelance journalist publishing across multiple newspapers while his electoral addresses for 1949 were at Maree, Griffith, Queensland and Toombul, Lilley, Queensland. One of his articles as 'services correspondent' for the *Brisbane Telegraph* on 3 May 1949, marked the celebration of the seven-year

---

103. Interviews with Craig Bensch, custodian of Frank's ventriloquist puppet, 2024–25. (H F Thoday collection)
104. 'New Baptist minister', *Port Lincoln Times*, 29 January 1953, 1.
105. 'Baptist', *The South Australian Government Gazette*, 30 August 1956, 503.
106. 'Local Couple's 12,000 mile phone call', *Port Lincoln Times*, 29 Jan 1959, 1.

anniversary of the Battle of the Coral Sea. Frank wrote with deep knowledge of the 1942 battle and promoted the importance of the collaboration between 'American and Australian services' throughout the Pacific War. He underlined the significance of this collaboration for 'saving Australia'.[107]

Frank was in Adelaide in the later months of 1949 prior to another overseas adventure. A newspaper article, 'S.A. man will study television abroad', published in the Adelaide *News* on 9 November 1949, provides some of the evidence for this.[108] The author of the article stated that Frank was holidaying with his parents at that time. The 'S.A. man', 'Mr Frank Courtis', was interviewed and his mission was summarised in the article. He was noted as 'a former Adelaide man who entered journalism after being invalided from the RAAF in 1944...'[109]

There remain no traces that this 'study' led to any tangible result for Australian broadcasters or audiences, despite his pioneering drive as outlined in the *News* article. Somehow, Frank managed to interweave this study with his employment at Black Star Publishing Company in London, from which he launched into his assignment as war correspondent during the Korean War.[110] Perhaps Frank's initial plan was overshadowed by the looming international unrest as well as his domestic concerns. While Frank was overseas in 1950, each of his parents suffered a stroke. Based on his past record of care for his parents, he may have returned to Australia during late 1950 to assist them.

---

107. Frank Courtis 'Coral Sea: Seven Years Ago History Was Made', *Brisbane Telegraph*, 3 May 1949, 4.
108. 'S.A. man will study television abroad', *News*, 9 November 1949, 20.
109. Ibid.
110. 'Black Star (photo agency)', *Wikipedia*, edited 30 December 2023.

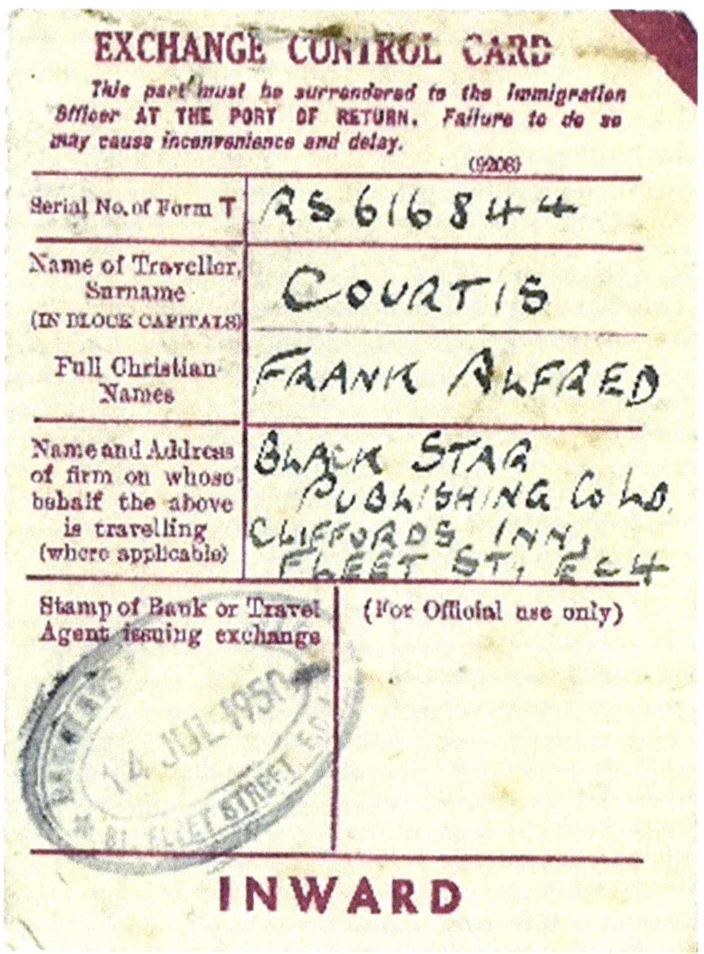

Exchange Control Card. (H F THODAY collection)

An Exchange Control Card, which has been in Bessie's family's possession, provides confirmation that Frank was employed by 'Black Star Publishing Co Ltd, Cliffords Inn, Fleet Street' from August 1950, indicating at least two synchronised roles at that time.

Black Star Publishing Company was established in December 1935 by three German Jews, Messrs Safranski, Mayer and Kornfeld, who fled Berlin during the Nazi regime. They carried new ideas and an innovative way of producing journalism that used page-sized photos and minimal text. This new style of journalism, or 'photojournalism', was emerging in the post-war 1940s. Black Star Publishing Company was housed at Cliffords Inn, Fleet Street, London, from the mid-1930s until the building's demolition in the headwinds of World War II. The entrance gate was retained and continues as a tourist landmark.[111]

Black Star Publishing Company began to service magazines in the United States of America, including *Life*, for whom Frank reportedly submitted photographs.[112] My extensive research has not revealed any photographs that Frank may have submitted for publication, although an article in *The Journalist*, an Australian publication, referred to Frank's freelance activities around 1950 and mentions that he had published in '*Illustrated London News* and other English magazines'.[113]

The Korean War began on 25 June 1950, when North Korea invaded South Korea across the 38th parallel, the latitudinal line that was used as the pre-Korean War boundary. The war ended in July 1953, with an armistice that left the peninsula divided. It seems that Frank's time in Korea as a war correspondent was short-lived, perhaps just a matter of six months or less in 1950. This may have been under the umbrella of the Black Star Publishing Company, London. *The Journalist*, a national journal of the Australian Journalists' Association, Melbourne, welcomed him into membership in January 1951, noting that he was a 'globetrotter': 'Frank went freelancing through Britain and Europe a couple of years ago. He ... just got out [of Korea] as the storm broke.'[114] Several decades later, Frank was heralded for his frank and fearless journalism, at that time, regarding the treatment of both young United States troops and Korean civilians.[115]

[111.] 'Cliffords Inn', *Wikipedia*, edited 21 March 2025.
[112.] 'Black Star (photo agency)', *Wikipedia*, op. cit. Black Star Publishing Company had connections with photojournalism, evident in Life magazine. Frank Courtis is mentioned in connection with Life as a Korean War journalist. However, I have not yet discovered any photographs or writing that he may have submitted to *Life*.
[113.] *The Journalist*, 1 January 1954, 4.
[114.] 'Press People', *The Journalist*, 1 January 1951, 4.
[115.] Mal Richardson, 'War correspondent – Korea – Part One', *Army*, 13 August 1981, 4.

Frank dressed for his journalist position at 'The Advertiser', photographed at Brighton, 1951. (H F Thoday collection)

Return to Adelaide

During early 1951 Frank had returned to Adelaide and was employed as a freelance journalist with *The Advertiser*. As mentioned, Frank registered as a new member of the Australian Journalists' Association who had 'joined the Adelaide *Advertiser* recently', having previously been employed by the *Brisbane Telegraph*. Despite his recent immersion on the North Korean front, Frank was able to passionately speak out in *The Journalist*, writing as pseudonym 'Aussie Freelance' from Landsborough, Queensland. He promoted the right of journalists to be paid a salary reflecting their 'after hours' work.[116]

At this time, Frank lived with his father at Elm Street, Brighton in South Australia, while his mother was unwell and a patient in hospital care for ten months. Both his father and mother had suffered a stroke in 1950 and were in poor health. As mentioned previously, it seems that Frank, their youngest child, provided strong care and support for his parents at this time.

An example of his wide repertoire of writing styles throughout his career included his critique of 'The Rivals' production at the Tivoli theatre in Adelaide, just days after admitting his mother to care.[117] This article intricately details Frank's knowledge of the original story and admiration for the artistic abilities of the contemporary performers.

On at least one occasion while living in Adelaide during 1951, Frank was invited to speak about his war-time experiences in connection with his spiritual beliefs. Frank was not a regular church attendee but indicated that he was 'Baptist' on his RAAF enlistment form. Frank's parents, Alfred and Min, attended their local Baptist church, and Frank occasionally accompanied them when he was holidaying at his parents' home. He was invited to speak at various venues across Adelaide, whenever he was staying at Brighton. One of these occasions was when he spoke to

---

[116.] 'Aussie Freelance', *The Journalist*, 1 January 1951, 4.
[117.] 'Rep. Success in Production of "The Rivals"', *The Advertiser*, 28 February 1951, 3.

a non-conformist Christian group at 'St Mary's A.W.U. [Australian Workers' Union] Hall, Flinders Street, [Adelaide] Sunday, 7 p.m.' and was introduced as 'a former war correspondent', speaking on the subject 'What Price Peace'.[118] Such an invitation to an A.W.U. venue in the high-Stalinist period of the Cold War, when peace was a 'dirty word', is further testimony to Frank's intellectual capacity and independent thinking. This capacity and independence gave him a critical perspective that transcended expedient clichés and the frozen political views of the day.[119]

Such an invitation to an A.W.U. venue in the high-Stalinist period of the Cold War, when peace was a 'dirty word', is further testimony to Frank's intellectual capacity and independent thinking.

Frank's mother, Min Courtis (born Emily Minnie Mary Elliott), died in Parkside Mental Hospital, on 5 November 1951, aged 79. This would have been a very difficult time for Frank, as he seemed to have been very close to his mother, enjoying her company and laughter. Occasions when this was evident included Frank's invitation to his parents to see him off on his Shell tour beginning in Albury in 1946, his return to his parents whenever he required recuperative care following war injuries, and when his parents moved house from Croydon Park to Brighton. He returned to his parents' home and visited his brother and sister and their families whenever he was on leave during the war and sent cards and bought gifts for all of his family. His understanding and reliability were evident when he accompanied his mother and completed forms for her admission into care in January 1951, ten months prior to her death, as well as his presence in Adelaide while she was in Parkside Mental Hospital

---

[118.] 'Advertising', *The Advertiser*, 21 July 1951, 13.
[119.] Kim Thoday, 'A harder thing than dying: peace activism and the Protestant Left in Australia during the early Cold War', in *Fighting Against War: Peace Activism in the Twentieth Century*, 2015, 241.

throughout 1951. Frank's father, Alfred, continued to live at Brighton until he passed away in residential care in 1960.

Frank continued his pursuit of wide-ranging interests after his mother's death and returned to Coffs Harbour. A mention in the 'Personal' column in the *Coffs Harbour Advocate* notes:

> *Widely-travelled newspaperman, Frank Courtis, is again visiting Coffs Harbour. Since his last visit four years ago, Frank has worked in Fleet Street and on the Continent. His last assignment was a coverage of the Korean War for 'Illustrated', London. Asked the reason for his present visit, Frank said 'because he is impressed with the district' and that speaks volumes for Coffs Harbour.[120]*

Identity

During the 1950s, Frank again appeared to be engaged in more than one employment role. My view is that he had various employment responsibilities integrated with communication and minor travel assignments. He appears to have been located across Australia and the Pacific, with connections to *The Bulletin*, Australian newspapers and the Defence Signals Branch. While his 'voice' in relation to signals intelligence had to be somewhat muted, his voice as a journalist was louder, opinionated and was often undersigned as 'Anonymous' or unsigned. One example of Frank's self-imposed stricture is his authorship of an article in the December 1953 issue of *The Journalist* where he was outspoken on the topic of payment for freelance journalists using the pseudonym 'Wondering'. During the early 1950s, Frank was a member of the Australian Journalists' Association (AJA). He anonymously advocated for himself and other journalists that casual rates should be applicable for those journalists who often worked out of hours, including at night.[121] As a self-declared 'new member' he was provocatively vocal.[122]

[120.] 'Personal', *Coffs Harbour Advocate*, 18 July 1952, 4.
[121.] 'Higher rates for casuals justified', *The Journalist*, December 1953, 4.
[122.] 'New members', ibid.

My research has revealed Frank's kaleidoscopic identity and multifaceted advocacy, visible through his many work locations throughout Australia's eastern states in communication roles. Another example is evident in January 1954, when Frank's 'Plea for the free-lance' was published in *The Journalist*. In this article, he argued that Australian writers, journalists and authors should provide the content of Australian newspapers and publications, so as to reflect Australian content.

Frank's multifaceted identity sets up a tantalising conundrum.

I would suggest that Frank's life as a journalist disguised his life as a Defence Signals Branch employee. An alternative explanation might be that he was employed as a signals staff member concurrently with being a journalist. This conundrum is tantalising and is yet to be more fully understood.

Photographer

True to his peripatetic life, but never to be easily stereotyped, Frank was off on another venture in April 1954. *The Courier-Mail* in Brisbane reported under their aptly titled 'Odd spot' that he was employed as a photographer on a forty-eight-foot launch, captained by Don Milne, which left Townsville as part of 'a survey of the commercial possibilities of the Barrier Reef'.[123]

There are no further traces of the success or otherwise of this venture, although this article refers to the potential for future expansion with a planned expedition utilising four vessels and the employment of scientists.[124]

More travels

More than twelve months later, in June 1955, Frank arrived at Outer Harbour, South Australia, aboard SS *Orontes*, having departed from Tilbury Docks, London. Frank had travelled as a

---

[123] 'Odd Spot', *The Courier-Mail*, 23 April 1954, 8.
[124] Ibid.

single passenger on this small single class passenger ship, owned by the Orient Line.[125] Presumably, Frank may have been in the United Kingdom or Europe during the more relaxed Cold War years of the mid-1950s, yet no traces nor photographs map his locations or roles.

125. 'Passenger arrivals', 'Incoming passenger list to Fremantle "Orontes" arrived 27 June 1955' 'Mr F Courtis', National Australian Archives, NAA: Series number K269, Item ID 30139419.

Family and Personal Passions

In September 1957, Frank's only sister, Bessie Dealy (nee Courtis), died in tragic circumstances. One photograph from this time includes Frank with his brother-in-law Albert (Bert) Dealy and Frank's father Alfred (Dick) Courtis. All three appear to have been engaged in garden or home maintenance. Frank again returned to the South Australian home of his father in Brighton and sister's family home in Hove during this time of grief and loss for all the family.

For further family occasions during 1958, 1960 and 1961, Frank may have also been residing and working in Adelaide. His niece Nancy Dealy married James Gwynne (Jim) Hodgetts on 25 March 1958. Frank's father died in 1960. Then his brother-in-law Albert passed away in mid-1961. Several months later, his niece Jenny Dealy married Gordon Evans on 21 October 1961 at St Jude's Church of England in Brighton, South Australia. Frank's parents, sister and nieces are memorialised at the St Jude's cemetery and cremation memorial wall. By November 1961, he had set off from his brother's house in Pooraka, South Australia, with a personal vision to promote water conservation, on a solo bicycle ride to Brisbane. *The Bulletin* referred to this as an escapade of an 'itinerant water-conserver, long-distance bike-rider' who was prone to undertaking unexpected enterprises.[126]

[126.] 'From Coffs Harbour to Higgins', *The Bulletin*, Vol 89, no 4589, 17 February 1968, 19, 20; interviews by Heather Thoday with Jenny Evans (nee Dealy), 1991–2025; interviews by Heather Thoday with Brian Smith, husband of Betty June Smith (nee Courtis), 2023–25.

Frank (far right) with his brother-in-law Albert Edward Dealy (centre) and father Alfred James Courtis (far left), about 1957. (H F Thoday collection)

Writing during the 1960s

The early 1960s reveal very little evidence of Frank's location or occupations. However, electoral records show that by 1963 he lived in Neutral Bay on the Lower North Shore of Sydney Cove in the Shire of Warringah, New South Wales. Neutral Bay is less than two kilometres from the Central Business District of Sydney. The electoral records indicate that he was employed as a journalist in the Shire of Ku-ring-gai at that time.

In June 1965, he applied for copyright for two literary works while living in William Street, Roseville, on the Upper North Shore of Sydney. His first literary work was a song poem, 'Can-can kangaroo'.[127] 'Can-can kangaroo' was not awarded copyright status. Contemporary readers may be unfamiliar with the energetic dance that underlies this song poem. Originally danced by couples between the World Wars, the dance evolved to essentially form a chorus-line performance, either all-female or all-male. The dance went through a stage of being scandalous, with dance steps that revealed female undergarments with high kicks. The can-can dance during the mid-twentieth century occasionally led to arrests. *Moulin Rouge* reportedly did not permit this type of performance.[128] The dance originated in France and was adapted internationally throughout the twentieth century, where perhaps Frank viewed it.

His other work, 'The touch of love', successfully copyrighted in October 1965, is overtly a love song, perhaps indicating a personal love interest. With metaphors and images depicting candle flame, fire and 'hearts ablaze', the poet evocatively asserts that his subject heats, warms, lights and keeps him young, through 'the touch of love'.

> **His other work, 'The touch of love', ... is overtly a love song, perhaps indicating a personal love interest.**

By September 1967 he was living at Woonona Avenue, Wahroonga, on the Upper North Shore of Sydney. In that year, Frank applied for copyright for a third literary work, 'Johnny Jacaranda', lodging it as a dramatic work.[129] With reference to Frank's third submitted work, the phrase 'Johnny Jacaranda' seems to derive from the Jacaranda tree. The Jacaranda seed, native to South America, was first imported and planted in the Brisbane Botanic Gardens in 1864. The seed was a gift by a South

---

[127] 'Author: Frank Alfred Courtis ... Can-can kangaroo ... 15 June 1965', National Archives of Australia, Location: Canberra, Series number A1336, Control symbol 66875, Item ID 4284843. 'Author: Frank Alfred Courtis ... The Touch of Love ... 29 June 1965', National Archives of Australia, Location: Canberra, Series number A1336, Control symbol 66916, Item ID 4284891. 'Author: Frank Alfred Courtis ... Johnny Jacaranda ... 26 September 1967', National Archives of Australia, Location: Canberra, Series number A1336, Control symbol Courtis F A, Item ID 5379552.
[128] 'Can-can', *Wikipedia*, page edited 20 March 2025.
[129] 'Johnny Jacaranda', op. cit.

American sea captain to the first superintendent of the Botanic Gardens, Walter Hill.[130] This poem links the seasonal changes of the Jacaranda with human emotion and concludes with the sadness of loss of Jacaranda foliage and of loss of a forbidden love.

I can find no trace of any prior publication of these works. Two of these three literary pieces are printed in full in 'Frank Courtis as Poet and Lyricist', in the postscript to this book.

After securing copyright for these literary works, according to a later biographical article in *The Bulletin*, Frank attempted to set up 'a mail-order book centre selling Australiana from his 'historic' property near Coffs Harbor'. Unfortunately, any further detail is elusive, but Frank did indicate, in a later interview while promoting his skill set, prior to the 1968 by-election, that his application was refused by the Australian Book Trading Advisory Council.[131]

Lost

According to a Statutory Declaration completed in July 1971, Frank 'lost the Certificate of Discharge [from the RAAF] … with my wallet and other personal papers at Coffs Harbour, NSW'. This certificate officially noted his number as 'A2102' and his rank as 'Squadron Leader' with a 'RAAF' unit. This loss occurred during New Year revelry on 1 January 1967. Accompanying the Statutory Declaration is a letter explaining that Frank 'reported [the loss] to the NSW Police at the time'.[132]

Federal by-election candidate

Frank decided to put his name forward for the electorate of Higgins, Melbourne, in the by-election held on 25 February 1968. The by-election was triggered by the drowning death of the

---

130. '10 places to go to find jacarandas blooming in Brisbane', Nature Play Queensland, https://natureplayqld.org.au/wp-content/uploads/2020/08/10_Places_to_go_to_find_Jacarandas_blooming_in_Brisbane.pdf.
131. 'From Coffs Harbor to Higgins', op cit., 20.
132. 'Statutory Declaration', Commonwealth of Australia, declared at Melbourne, 21 July 1971, one page. 'Letter addressed to Officer in Charge, Records Section, Department of Air, Russell Offices, Canberra, ACT, 14 July 1971. 'Courtis, Frank Alfred', National Archives of Australia. NAA: A8877, 15318553.

Australian Prime Minister, Harold Holt in December 1967. Frank's multifaceted platform reflected his eclectic interests which included nationalism, social justice praxis and advocating for democratic rights for everyday Australians. The *Bulletin* noted that he was 'interested in promoting free enterprise, justice for the aged, an Australian shipping line and the conservation of natural resources and water [as well as] … Australia's relations with the rest of the world'.[133]

Frank made use of his penchant for theatrics in the pre-election campaign to seek attention to his political views. Clearly, he received media attention for this, as is evident in numerous newspaper accounts at the time. These accounts sometimes ridiculed his playful approach. Nevertheless, Frank's political astuteness was revealed when he satirically presented himself as the underdog and deployed a creative prank in the hope of securing a 'donkey vote' in the election.[134] So Frank purchased a donkey, added a blue ribbon around DooLittle's neck, and paraded the animal in the streets of the Higgins electorate.

Frank's penchant for theatrics often led to misunderstood or ridiculed messaging

Another politicised prank highlighted the ever-present possibility that Frank's messaging could be misunderstood or ridiculed. In such a vein, his application for setting up a campaign tent in a Malvern parkland was officially unsuccessful. However, not to be dissuaded, Frank appeared happy to be snapped by local media as he cheekily hammered in the tent pegs. These vibrant and subversive personality traits were clearly visible in a photograph that is currently held at the State Library of Victoria.[135]

---

[133] 'From Coffs Harbor to Higgins', op. cit., 20.

[134] See proliferation of articles in early 1968, such as: 'Rescuer of PM now his rival', *Sunday Mail*, January 1968, no page (see H F Thoday collection); 'He's hoping for the donkey vote', *The Canberra Times*, 6 February 1968, 1; 'Mr Gorton to be spectator', *The Canberra Times*, 24 February 1968, 3.

[135] Photograph held by State Library of Victoria, 'Frank Courtis', contributor, *Herald and Weekly Times*, c. 1968, In copyright, Herald & Weekly Times Limited

Frank ran as an Independent in the by-election and scored fourth place in the results with over three hundred votes in the blue-ribbon seat of Higgins. John Gorton, the incumbent Prime Minister, won the by-election.

portrait collection, Accession no H28849/5281, donated by Herald and Weekly Times Limited 1977, Record ID 9917824073607636.

Military Traces

In July 1971, four years after Frank had lost his wallet and valuable papers in Coffs Harbour, his RAAF 'Certificate of Discharge' was resupplied and 'F.J. Green, the Secretary, Department of Air, Russell Offices, Canberra', informed him that:

> *Medals will be inscribed with your service particulars and forwarded as soon as they are received from the engravers. The uninscribed campaign stars previously issued will also be engraved if returned under registered cover …*

Frank's five medals and one badge are listed in his Military War Record held at the National Archives of Australia:[136]

1939-45 Star
Pacific Star
Defence Medal
War Medal 1939–45
Australia Service Medal 1939–45
Returned from Active Service Badge

The Department of Defence recently confirmed that Frank was issued with the 1939-45 Star and Pacific Star medals.[137] Document-

---

[136.] 'Courtis, Frank Alfred', National Archives of Australia. NAA NAA A8877, 15318553. Note that years are varioulsy annotated in official documentation, primarily as 1939-45. My use of '1939-45' reflects the documentation. However, when I am directly referring to the photographed medals, '1939-1945' reflects the inscription on each medal.

[137.] The Department of Defence indicated that the two Star medals were issued to

ation held in Frank's war service record at the National Archives of Australia indicates that these two medals were scribed with Frank's name and service number on the back. As these two medals were issued and lost, Frank's extended family have purchased replicas, photographs of which are included below. The Defence Medal, War Medal 1939-45 and the Australia Service Medal 1939-45 were not issued to Frank during his lifetime. Frank's extended family have subsequently been issued with these three medals, photographs of which are also included below.

The 1939-1945 Star awarded to Frank Alfred Courtis, Service No. 2102, replica purchased posthumously, January 2026. (H F Thoday collection)

1939-45 Star

All air crew who had actively served for two months or more in an operational unit were awarded the 1939–45 Star. Note that Frank was among those who were in Malaya between 8 December 1941 and 15 February 1942, at the time of the 'Fall of Singapore'. Those troops who were in Malaya and escaped as Frank did, aboard MV *Derrymore*, were also automatically awarded the Pacific Star.

Frank post-war. See the letter from the Department of Defence to Heather Thoday, 28 August 2025. These two medals were subsequently lost by Frank.

The Pacific Star awarded to Frank Alfred Courtis, Service No. 2102, replica purchased posthumously, January 2026.
(H F Thoday collection)

Pacific Star

The Pacific Star was awarded for active service in the Pacific region from 8 December 1941 and 2 September 1945. It was also awarded, in addition to the 1939–45 Star, for participation in certain special operations in the Pacific region.

The Defence Medal awarded to Frank Alfred Courtis, Service No. 2102, issued posthumously, November 2025. (H F Thoday collection)

Defence Medal

The Defence Medal was awarded for:

• six months of service in a prescribed non-operational area subject to enemy air attack or closely threatened in Australia and overseas

• twelve months of non-operational service in defence forces overseas deployed from or outside Australia.

Within Australia, the qualifying area was the Northern Territory, north of 14 degrees 30 minutes south, and the Torres Strait Islands. The qualifying period was between 3 September 1939 and 2 September 1945.

Overseas service included the Middle East, east of the Suez Canal (less the period of the Syrian Campaign) or Malaya prior to the Japanese invasion on 8 December 1941.[138]

[138.] Frank's eligibility was due to his deployment in diverse roles from 1939 to 1945, mainly in the Pacific region and overseas. https://www.defence.gov.au/adf-members-families/honours-awards/imperial-awards/australia-service-medal-1939-1945.

*The War Medal 1939-1945,
awarded to Frank Alfred Courtis,
Service No. 2102, issued
posthumously, November 2025.
(H F Thoday collection)*

War Medal 1939-45

The War Medal 1939–1945 was awarded for twenty-eight days full-time service in the armed forces between 3 September 1939 and 2 September 1945.[139]

[139.] https://www.defence.gov.au/adf-members-families/honours-awards/imperial-awards/war-medal-1939-1945; https://militaryshop.com.au/products/war-medal-1939-1945. As noted previously, my use of '1939-45' reflects the documentation. However, when I am directly referring to the photographed medals, '1939-1945' reflects the inscription on each medal.

The Australia Service Medal 1939-1945, awarded to Frank Alfred Courtis, Service No. 2102, issued posthumously, November 2025. (H F Thoday collection)

Australia Service Medal 1939-45

The Australia Service Medal 1939–1945 was awarded for either at least eighteen months' full-time service or at least three years' part-time service at any period during World War II.

Returned from Active Service Badge

'The purpose of the Returned from Active Service Badge (RASB) is to recognise Australian Defence Force members who have returned from active or warlike service during military campaigns in operational areas.' The RASB is worn on civilian clothing. Frank's badge has been lost and no purchase of a replica has been pursued by the family.[140]

Two medals, the 1939-45 Star and the Pacific Star, may have been in Frank's safe keeping at least until the end of his residence at Umina Beach, New South Wales. At the time of Frank's death almost twenty years later, with the dispersal of his possessions and estate, they were again lost. Further, as stated in a recent letter a representative of the Directorate of Honours and Awards, Department of Defence, Frank was not issued with the Defence Medal, War Medal 1939-45 or Australia Service Medal 1939-45 during his lifetime.[141] Successfully gathering these traces of Frank's military life have broadened understandings and confirmed aspects of his previously uncharted journeys throughout his military career. Navigating the curiosities of the loss of two medals and a badge, as well as the non-issue of three of the medals, has added to the unanswered questions that typically signify the narrative of Frank's life.

[140.] The Returned from Active Service Badge may have been worn on those occasions when he was invited to speak at Christian Churches, such as St Mary's non-conformist group in July 1951. The Advertiser, 21 July 1951, 13. https://www.defence.gov.au/adf-members-families/honours-awards/australian-awards/returned-active-service-badge.

[141.] Letter from J Williams, Assessor, Veterans and Families Section, Service Awards and Medal Management, Directorate of Honours and Awards, Department of Defence, 28 August 2025.

'Dunstan decade'[142]

Among the chaotic mix of lodging his literary works for copyright, chasing his lost wallet with his RAAF Certificate of Discharge and military medals at Coffs Harbour, his defeat in the 1968 by-election and being present at his youngest niece Betty's wedding to Brian Smith in Adelaide, Frank introduced his partner to his brother, his niece and her husband. As can be seen from the photographs depicting Frank with unnamed male friends, his relationships were evidently embraced by some of his family. Frank's male partner was warmly accepted into the family and this relationship lasted for at least a decade throughout the sixties and much of the seventies. South Australia's beachside suburbs became places where Frank and his partner visited

South Australia was the first Australian state to decriminalise homosexuality.

and holidayed often. Their lifestyle was more sustainable within the liberal culture that Premier Don Dunstan promoted.

Throughout the late 1960s and 1970s, South Australia offered and embraced radical social changes, marked by increasing possibilities regarding socio-politically sensitive areas such as sexuality. South Australia was the first Australian state to decriminalise homosexuality, with legislation being passed in 1975. New South Wales did not pass this legislation until 1984.[143]

[142.] 'Dunstan decade' refers to the years in the late 1960s and 1970s when Don Dunstan was most influential in South Australian legislation, politics and culture. Angela Woollacott is one of many biographers and commentators who utilise this term. Angela Woollacott, Don Dunstan: *The Visionary Politician Who Changed Australia*, 2019.
[143.] Ibid., 175, 259.

Unfortunately, none of Frank's artefacts are available from this time. One living family member who recalls these visits, cannot recall Frank's partner's name. Nor are there photographs, letters, cards, or other tangible traces of Frank's presence from this decade.

The family member recounts that Frank and his partner often holidayed with his brother's family in South Australia. Norman's work as an adult technical educator required him to travel to regional areas, so he and his wife would take their caravan during his work contracts. Frank and his partner would often meet up with the family on holidays to Stansbury and be accommodated as guests at Frank's brother's and niece's homes.[144] Frank's earlier experience of being injured and afloat in water had not dampened his enthusiasm for water sports.

Fishing and boating, along with caravanning and camping, remained recreational experiences that Frank shared with Norman and his brother's family. Frank and Norman were co-owners of a fishing boat which was continuously moored at Stansbury. The boat eventually sank while moored in St Vincent's Gulf. This coast had been significant for the family for many years, as Norman and Frank's father, Alfred, was born at Ardrossan. Previous to Frank's lifetime, his paternal grandparents had unsuccessfully attempted to farm in the region during the 1880s drought. They lived through to the 1920s and had been a part of Frank's life until his mid-teens.

[144.] Norman and Gwen Courtis were noted as holidaymakers at Stansbury Caravan Park, where Frank also often holidayed with them during the 1950s to 1970s. 'Notes about people', *Pioneer*, 12 January 1951, 3.

Later life

Electoral records reveal that Frank lived mainly in Victoria in the early 1970s. However, consistent with Frank's wandering lifestyle, he resided in Honolulu for two months in the winter of 1970, either for recreational or work purposes. Honolulu, the capital of Hawaii, is only eight miles from Pearl Harbor. Having resided in Honolulu for two months, Frank returned to Australia when his ship docked in Queensland in September 1970.[145] By 1971 he is recorded as living in a 'flat' in Inkerman Street, St Kilda, Victoria. In 1972 he was residing at another 'flat' in Acland Street, St Kilda. It may not have been a coincidence that the Defence Signals Branch was in the same suburb.

Frank's long-term partner was killed in a motorbike accident during 1978.[146] During several conversations with a male family member whose camaraderie with Frank during the 1960s through to the late 1970s was evident, we talked about Frank's devastation following his partner's death and Frank's angst about whether to return to live in South Australia. Frank looked at several South Australian properties and ultimately decided to continue living at Umina Beach in New South Wales.

There are scant remaining traces of Frank's adventures during the late 1970s and 1980s, the last decades of his life. He may have continued to be employed with the Department of Defence until he

---

145. 'Incoming passenger cards – July – December 1970', 'Passenger listing', 'Mr Frank Alfred Courtis', National Australian Archives, NAA: Series number: A1197, Item ID 12257055.
146. Interviews by Heather Thoday with Brian Smith, op. cit., 2023–25.

*Frank, near Stansbury, South Australia, no date,
c. 1975, photographed by Smith family.
(H F Thoday collection)*

turned sixty-five years of age in 1979, while simultaneously continuing freelance journalism.

Rachel Noble, previous Director-General of the Australian Signals Directorate writes about the unique place of 'The Factory' in history:[147]

[147.] The term 'the factory' evolved as signals were captured and processed by amateurs in Australia, enabling informed strategic decisions to be applied in war zones, such as the South-West Pacific area. The informally-named factory

In July 1979, when the newly renamed Defence Signals Directorate finally moved to its new purpose-built accommodation in Victoria Barracks, the Minister for Defence, The Hon. James Killen, sent this encouraging message:

We cannot talk about the activities of the Directorate. The national interest, and, indeed, the wider interest of civilised mankind, sweep you to silence. Can I say that in the years to come our people will look back with gratitude to you for your devotion.[148]

This year, 2022, the Australian Signals Directorate commemorates 75 years of serving the people of Australia and is taking this opportunity to cast aside some of our silence to tell our story to the Australian public we serve.'

This story has never been told, because in the secret world we could not, and cannot, share what we do all day, even with family and loved ones.[149]

Carrying the unique weight of his life experience, Frank probably retired on his sixty-fifth birthday in August 1979 and finally settled in 1980 at his house at Palm Tree Grove, Umina Beach.

Frank was once described in an article in *The Bulletin* as:

… a journalist, war correspondent, fitter and engineer, trade publicity officer, ardent nationalist, itinerant water-conserver, long-distance bike rider, and associated with aid for refugees and food for Asia schemes.[150]

The article adds that he was an election campaigner, local entrepreneur and book marketing applicant. These multiple layers

---

became highly regarded for the contributions to the international 'five eyes' signals intelligence arena. 'The factory' has been formalised and re-shaped during the ensuing decades, from the Defence Signals Branch in 1947, to the current Australian Signals Directorate.

[148.] Inwards ships passenger manifest, Location: Brisbane, 1 August 1970, National Archives of Australia: mp/ B{264/, 5082701.

[149.] Rachel Noble in Fahey, *The Factory*, op. cit., vii.

[150.] 'From Coffs Harbor to Higgins', *The Bulletin*, op. cit., 17 Feb 1968, 20.

*Frank, Umina Beach, October 1979, photographed by
Jenny Evans. (H F Thoday collection)*

of Frank's experience were achieved by the time that he was fifty-three years of age. From the artefacts that I have gathered, I can also add military intelligence officer, poet, author of literary works, ventriloquist, puppeteer, entertainer and photographer to this list. Frank was certainly keen to have a go at a multitude of experiences and promoted causes in which he sincerely believed. Many of these fervent interests continued to drive him throughout his life.

Later life

In October 1979, one of Frank's nieces, Jenny, her husband Gordon and two of their children, Steven and Michelle, briefly visited him at his home in Umina Beach. He had just celebrated his sixty-fifth birthday and retired that year.

A decade later, in mid-1989, Frank's brother, Norman and Norman's wife, Gwen, drove from Adelaide to visit Frank in his home in Umina Beach. Norman and Frank had verbally agreed that Norman would assist Frank to sort through his belongings, perhaps in preparation to move to more manageable accommodation. Unfortunately, Norman and Gwen had a major car accident and were inpatients at Orange Hospital for a significant time, before returning to Adelaide. Frank was not seen by family members again.

Umina Beach, 1980. (H F Thoday collection)

Frank Alfred Courtis died on 19 October 1989 at seventy-five years of age at Restwell Nursing Home at Strathfield, New South Wales. Frank had been admitted by a neighbour and friend, when his Alzheimer's disease had prevented him from continuing to live safely at home. His end-of-life request ensured that his ashes were scattered at Umina Beach. There are no further traces to mark the passing of Frank's life.

Looking back at photographs of Frank, he can be viewed either on the sandy beachfront with his family or among the coconut palms of Darwin or seated on the sand with a typewriter balanced on his legs, and it can be seen that he was at ease near any beach or coastline. His ordeal in the sea at the fall of Singapore did not seem to affect his love of the beach, sand or seaside. His own words, as a war correspondent near Rabaul, seem apt as a closing description of his worldview of humanity and the significance of beach views:

> *And so we move back towards the beach area back through the ruins of Rabaul consumed by jungle with colored [sic] patches of frangipanni and bougainvilla [sic] showing the remains of what were residents gardens ... And so the sun sets and Rabaul is transformed again into a place of beauty[.] The houses can be built again and the avenue of trees rejuvenated[.] The encroaching jungle can be conquered[.] For nature has a way with her that man made bombs can not destroy[.] There still remains a scenic harbor [sic] flanked by rugged hills[.] The ground has been torn and scarred but the good earth will still produce[.] ends Courtis[151]*

[151.] Courtis, dispatch, 12 September 1945. My capitalisation at sentence beginnings, with my full stops at end of sentences.

Epilogue

On Thursday 25 January 1990, a notice regarding Frank Alfred Courtis's estate was published in the Government Gazette of the State of New South Wales.[152] The notice indicated the Supreme Court of New South Wales ruled that the 'probate of the Will dated 18th December, 1979' was granted to the Public Trustee on 12 January 1990.

At the time of the distribution of Frank's estate, financial assets were the only traces that remained. All further documentation, photographs or other traces had been lost.

---

[152] *Government Gazette of the State of New South Wales*, no 14, 25 Jan 1990, 755.

Afterword

When I began gathering the scattered and often obscure remnants of Frank's life, following the realisation that no other physical mementos had been retained, I became further inspired to link these elusive fragments. My search for further traces continues as further sources for research become available, including:

- seeking more information about his assignment to Black Star Publishing Company in London in the later 1940s
- seeking further details from *Illustrated London News* for articles or photographs connected to 1950 when he was reportedly a war correspondent during the Korean War
- discovering further details about his relationships or connections within the RAAF and Australian Journalists' Association

and uncovering and understanding further traces of the life of Frank Alfred Courtis.

Bibliography

H F Thoday Collection: Certificates, Photographs, Letters, Oral Recounts

Birth certificate of Jean Courtis, 27 June 1905, Boulder, Western Australia.

Interviews by Heather Thoday, with Jenny Evans (nee Dealy), 1991–2025.

Interviews by Heather Thoday, with Brian Smith, husband of Betty June Smith (nee Courtis), 2023–25.

Interviews by Heather Thoday, with Craig Bensch, custodian of Frank's ventriloquist puppet, 2024–25.

Letter from Mercy Lawrie (nee Payne) to Jenny Evans (nee Dealy), 16 September 1991.

Letter from Frank Courtis to his nieces Nancy Dealy and Jenny Dealy, November 1943.

Letter from Allison Augustine, Director, Defence Honours and Awards, People Services and Wellbeing, Department of Defence, to Dr Heather Thoday, 4 November 2025.

Letter from J Williams, Assessor, Veterans and Families Section, Service Awards and Medal Management, Directorate of Honours and Awards, Department of Defence, to Dr Heather Thoday, 28 August 2025.

Marriage certificate of Alfred James Courtis and Emily Minnie Mary Elliott, 13 July 1904, Kalgoorlie, Western Australia.

Photographs of the Courtis family held in the Courtis family collection, 1917–87.

Telegram from Frank Courtis to his sister Bessie Dealy, December 1943.

Books

Bridge, Carl, 'Allies of a kind: Three wartime Australian ministers to the United States, 1940-46', in *Australia Goes to Washington: 75 Years of Australian Representation in the United States 1940-2015*, (eds) David Lowe, Carl Bridge, David Lee, ANU Press, Acton, Australia, 2016.

Dufty, David, *The Secret Code-breakers of Central Bureau: How Australia's Signals-intelligence Network helped win the Pacific War*, Scribe, Brunswick, 2017.

Fahey, John, *The Factory: The Official History of the Australian Signals Directorate.* Vol 1, Allen & Unwin, Crows Nest, 2023.

Flanagan, Richard, *The Narrow Road to the Deep North*, Vintage Books, North Sydney, 2013.

Thoday, Heather, *Courtis Lines in South Australia*, Staurolite Publications, Gawler, 2024.

Thoday, Kim, 'A harder thing than dying: Peace activism and the Protestant Left in Australia during the early Cold War' in *Fighting Against War: Peace Activism in the Twentieth Century,* (eds) Phillip Deery and Julie Kimber, Leftbank Press, Melbourne, 2015, 224-245.

Woollacott, Angela, *Don Dunstan: The Visionary Politician Who Changed Australia*, Allen & Unwin, Crows Nest, 2019.

Newspapers, Gazettes, Journals

The Advertiser (Adelaide, SA: 1889–1931).

The Advertiser (Adelaide, SA: 1931–1954).

Advocate (Melbourne, Victoria: 1868–1954).

Age (Melbourne, Victoria: 1854–1954).

Air Force News (National: 1941).

Army (National: 1980–2021).

Army News, (Darwin, NT: 1941–1946).

The Australian Monthly Motor Manual, Vol. 1, No. 5, August 1946, 'More petrol and the touring season is on', 22.

Australian Church Record, no 1409, 21 March 1968.

Border Morning Mail (Albury, NSW: 1946).

Bibliography

Brisbane Telegraph (Brisbane, Qld: 1948–1954).
The Bulletin, Vol 61, no 3168 (30 October 1940).
The Bulletin, Vol 89, no 4589 (17 Feb 1968).
The Canberra Times (Canberra, ACT: 1926–1995).
Centralian Advocate (Alice Springs, NT: 1947–1954).
Cloncurry Advocate (Qld: 1931–1953).
Coffs Harbour Advocate (NSW: 1907–1942;1946–1954).
Commonwealth of Australia Gazette (National: 1901–1973).
The Courier-Mail (Brisbane, Qld: 1933–1954).
Daily News (Perth, WA: 1882–1955).
Government Gazette of the State of New South Wales, no 14, 25 Jan 1990.
The Journalist, Newspaper of Australian Journalists Association,
    Collins Street, Melbourne (Melbourne, Victoria: 1910–1954).
The Mail (Adelaide, SA: 1912–1954).
News (Adelaide, SA: 1923–1954).
Northern Champion (Taree, NSW: 1913-1954).
Northern Standard (Darwin, NT: 1921–1955).
Pioneer (Yorketown, SA: 1898 – 1954).
Port Lincoln Times (SA:1927–1965;1992–2002).
The Register News–Pictorial (Adelaide, SA:1929–1931).
The South Australian Government Gazette, no 41, 30 August 1956.
The South Australian Genealogist, Vol 51, no 3, August 2024, Thoday,
    Heather and Window, Joy, 'These shoes were made for walking',
    18–24.
Sun News-Pictorial (Melbourne, Victoria: 1922–1954;1956).
Sunday Mail (Adelaide, SA: 1912–1968).
Unknown publisher, McCarron, Bird & Company, Printers, 479
    Collins Street, Melbourne, no date, '10,000 mile tour', no page
    number.

Documents accessed at Australian War Memorial and National Archives of Australia

Australian War Memorial
'Brisbane, Qld, 1945-07, officers of the Central Bureau of

intelligence at Archerfield Aerodrome', Australian War Memorial/Collection, Photograph, accession number P0437. Original housed in AWM Private Records Collection at P0437/12/10. (Courtesy of National Archives of Australia: P01443.045) (Retrieved September 2025)

'Malaguna Mission, New Britain, 1945-09-10. War correspondents typing their stories on the beach', Australian War Memorial/ Collection, accession number 096287. (Courtesy of Australian Army History Unit, Department of Defence) (Retrieved September 2025)

SIS Record Association, *Special intelligence service in the Far East, 1942-1946: an historical and pictorial record*, SIS Record Association, Brooklyn, New York,1946.

National Archives of Australia

'Author: Frank Alfred Courtis … Can-can kangaroo … 15 June 1965', Location: Canberra, Series number A1336, Control symbol 66875, Item ID 4284843. (Content courtesy of H F Thoday collection: courtesy of F A Courtis estate)

'Author: Frank Alfred Courtis … The Touch of Love … 29 June 1965', Location: Canberra, Series number A1336, Control symbol 66916, Item ID 4284891. (Content courtesy of H F Thoday collection: courtesy of F A Courtis estate)

'Author: Frank Alfred Courtis … Johnny Jacaranda … 26 September 1967', Location: Canberra, Series number A1336, Item ID 5379552. (Content courtesy of H F Thoday collection: courtesy of F A Courtis estate)

'Courtis, Frank Alfred: Service number 2102, Date of birth 13 August 1914, Place of birth Croydon SA, Place of enlistment Laverton, Next of kin, Courtis A', Location: Melbourne, Series number A8877, Item ID 15318553.

'Courtis, Frank Alfred, War Correspondent 422', Location: Melbourne, Series number B4717, Item ID 30107811.

'Statutory Declaration', Commonwealth of Australia, declared at Melbourne, 21 July 1971, one page. 'Letter addressed to Officer in Charge, Records Section, Department of Air, Russell Offices, Canberra, ACT, 14 July 1971. 'Courtis, Frank Alfred: Service number 2102, Date of birth 13 August 1914, Place of birth Croydon SA, Place of enlistment Laverton, Next of kin, Courtis A', Location: Melbourne, Series number A8877, Item ID 15318553, unnumbered page.

Department of External Territories [1], Central Office, 'Instrument of Surrender – surrender of all Japanese Armed Forces in Papua New Guinea', signed on board HMS Glory, Rabaul Harbour, 6 September 1945.

'Office procedure and instruction at RAAF representative Washington', National Archives of Australia, Contents range 1943-1946, p 3. (Image courtesy of National Archives of Australia. NAA: A1695, 6/303/ORG, 139382.) (Retrieved October 2025)

'Passenger arrivals', 'Incoming passenger cards – July – December 1970', 'Mr Frank Alfred Courtis', National Australian Archives, NAA: Series number: A1197, Item ID 12257055. (Retrieved December 2024)

'Passenger arrivals', 'Incoming passenger list to Fremantle "Orontes" arrived 27 June 1955' 'Mr F Courtis', National Australian Archives, NAA: Series number K269, Item ID 30139419. (Retrieved December 2024)

'Press – war correspondents Frank Courtis – Despatches after the capture of Rabaul *(Aug-Sep 1945)*', Location: Australian War Memorial, Series number AWM54, Control symbol 773/4/87, Item ID 473986. (Courtesy of Australian Army History Unit, Department of Defence) (Retrieved July 2024)

'Volume 2 – Number 6 RAAF Hospital – Personnel Occurrence Report 1/1944 – 125/1944' 03 Jan 1944 – 11 Aug 1944, National Archives of Australia, Series number A1060k5, Control symbol 558/3, Item ID 30677383. (Image courtesy of National Archives of Australia. NAA: A1060k5, 30677383.) (Retrieved October 2025)

Websites and Blogs

'10 places to go to find jacarandas blooming in Brisbane', Nature Play Queensland, https://natureplayqld.org.au. (Retrieved April 2025)

'12 Squadron History, RAAF': 'Deployment to Darwin', 'Introduction', 'Operations in the tropics – 1939', *Australian military aviation history*, The Australian Military Aviation History Association, no date. https://raafdocumentary.com. (Retrieved April 2025)

Atalanta passenger list, April 1866, London and Plymouth to Adelaide, https://web.archive.org/web/20240813092428/http://www.theshipslist.com. (Retrieved June 2025)

'Fisher, Cec, 'An original member of 12 Squadron RAAF, his stories and photographic collection'. www.ozatwar.com/raaf/cecfisher.htm (Retrieved November 2024)

'Gulumoerrgin Larrakia seasons calendar', https://nesplandscapes.edu.au/wp-content/uploads/2016/10/Gulumoerrgin-Larrakia-seasons-calendar.pdf. (Retrieved April 2025)

Hansen, Leslie W, 'MV Derrymore glass negative', Collections Online, Amgueddfa Cymru – Museum Wales, no date. https://museum.wales/collections/online/object/4d957b22-c1e1-33ff-a2b3-c01e71e3f07c/MV-Derrymore-glass-negative. (Retrieved September 2025)

'Honours and Awards', Australian Government, Department of Defence, ADF members and families, www.defence.gov.au. (Retrieved June 2025)

'Pacific Wrecks', 1995-2025, www.pacificwrecks.com. (Retrieved April 2025)

'Passengers in history' online project, South Australian Maritime Museum, Photograph sourced from South Australian Maritime Museum. (Retrieved 1 March 2025)

State Library of Victoria Photograph held by State Library of Victoria 'Frank Courtis', contributor, *Herald and Weekly Times*, ca. 1968, In copyright, Herald & Weekly Times Limited portrait collection, accession no H28849/5281, donated by Herald and

Bibliography

Weekly Times Limited 1977, Record ID 9917824073607636.

State Records of South Australia, 'Record of employment sheets - South Australian Railways' GRS 10638, Rail Commissioner, Series Date Range 1880-1976, Index Q-T, 29 September 2021. (Retrieved June 2025)

The Australian Military Shop, Fyshwick, Australian Capital Territory, https://militaryshop.com.au. (Retrieved June 2025)

Window, Joy and Thoday, Heather (Administrators), *Courtis Connections*, blog, https://courtisconnections.wordpress.com. (Retrieved May 2025)

Australian Government Department of Foreign Affairs and Trade

'Historical documents', '145 Churchill to Curtin', Cablegram Winch 6 London, 27 March 1943, 9.25 p.m., www.dfat.gov.au. (Retrieved March 2025)

'Historical documents', '152 Dixon to Curtin', Cablegram 571 Washington, 6 April 1943, 6.33 p.m., www.dfat.gov.au. (Retrieved March 2025)

Wikipedia pages

'Allied Intelligence Bureau', *Wikipedia*, edited 23 July 2024. (Retrieved 19 February 2025)

'Australian New Guinea Administrative Unit', *Wikipedia*, edited 18 January 2025. (Retrieved 19 February 2025)

'Black Star (photo agency)', *Wikipedia*, edited 30 December 2023. (Retrieved 30 December 2024)

'Caleb Grafton Roberts', *Wikipedia*, edited 10 November 2024. (Retrieved 19 February 2025)

'Can-can', *Wikipedia*, edited 20 March 2025. (Retrieved 1 April 2025)

'Cliffords Inn' *Wikipedia*, edited 21 March 2025. (Retrieved 1 May 2025)

'Frank Marshall (puppeteer)', *Wikipedia*, edited 20 June 2024. (Retrieved 12 March 2025)

'John Gorton'. *Wikipedia*, edited 20 September 2025. (Retrieved 30
    September 2025)

Appendix: Frank Courtis as Poet and Lyricist

This appendix holds two published and two copyrighted works only. The first two poems were written by Frank and published in national and New South Wales publications in 1940 and 1942. Further, the two pieces of literary and dramatic works are held in the National Australian Archives (NAA) and were successfully registered with copyright from 1965 and 1967 respectively. A third literary work was unsuccessful in gaining registration for copyright in 1965 and has not been included here. It is available for viewing at the NAA website.

Australia abroad[153]

Give them their thoughts of Home when they have seen
Long shadows on the sand merge into night;
Let them dream on and think of what has been
Back in their southern land; let them delight
In memories of breakers on the shore,
The curling smoke of campfires in the night,
The kookaburra's laugh, the eerie light
The dust-pall brings, the way the eagles soar.

For dawn shall dye that ancient desert red,
And mystic, hallowed sands be richer far
Because they passed that way – by freedom led.
Dreams were the seeds they sowed, and naught shall mar
The flower of faith that from their dreaming springs;
Tended and nurtured long by loving hands,
Fed by warm streams of life on sunkissed sands,
It must live on, and grow, and spread its wings.

It must live on to shade an ageing world
Blinded by bitter hate; and nations small
Torn by the lust for power, and legions hurled
In blind obedience to a leader's call.
Youth knows no hates like these; its sky of stars
Illumines all the earth; its chivalry
Forces it onward like a flowing sea,
To smooth the sands of time and heal its scars.

Give them their thoughts of Home, and let them see
Further than flitting visions on the sand
Further than death itself. Their destiny
Is sure; with deathless honor [sic], hand in hand,

---

153. *The Bulletin*, vol 61, no 3168, 30 October 1940, 35.

They face a changing world which they must mould.
Give them their dreams; give them the vision clear
Of freedom in a land where life is dear,
And laughter dearer far than power or gold.
Frank A. Courtis

The call[154]

Our bloodless sands, encircled by the sea,
Have not yet felt a foreign tyrant's heel;
Sun-warmed they live, the playground of the free;
Star-lit by night when evening shadows steal,
And wandering from the east, engulf the land
Silent and still beneath the Southern sky.
Save where the breakers murmur on the sand,
Or night birds stir the leaves as they pass by.
And yet, in all this stillness comes a sound,
The echo of a far-flung Empire's cry,
Growing until it rocks the very ground,
It rouses us from dull complacency.
Oh England! we are coming, young and strong –
Freedom our battle cry, and love our song.
Frank A. Courtis, RAAF.

---

[154] First published in *The Sydney Morning Herald* (NSW: 1842–1954), Saturday 30 November 1940, 11. Further published in *The Northern Champion* (Taree, NSW: 1913–1954), Wednesday 22 April 1942, 4.

The touch of love[155]

The touch of love is a touch of gladness,
The touch of love is a touch of sadness,
The touch of love is a candle bright –
It can shine through the dark, it can set you alight,
So darling love me right.

When I'm holding your hand
There's a feeling so grand
That comes stealing;
It warms me inside
Like a newly-wed bride,
What a feeling!

I could cry when I'm glad,
I could sing when I'm sad
When you're near me;
I feel hot when I'm cold,
I'll feel young when I'm old,
Stay with me.

You have started a fire,
You have kindled desire
In my heart, dear;
You're a fireman at heart,
You will tear me apart
If we part, dear.

With hearts both ablaze
We shall truly amaze,

[155.] 'The touch of love' was submitted as a 'song lyric' for registration of copyright on 29 June 1965. Registration of copyright was granted on 15 July 1965. Application papers and poem are open for view, NAA, Series number A1336, Control symbol 66916, Item ID. 4284891.

Do not slight me;
Your touch means so much,
There's such fire in your touch
Darling light me.

Appendix: Frank Courtis as Poet and Lyricist

Johnny Jacaranda[156]

Johnny Jacaranda,   Girl sings
Johnny Johnny Jac …
I am waiting lonely
For the waves to bring you back,
I am for you only
And the sun is sinking low …
Oh Johnny Jacaranda,
Why did you have to go?

This is Johnny's board-bird -   Boy speaks, matter of fact
He met her on the sand.
They rode the waves together
Walked the surf's edge hand-in-hand.
He had hair that turned to yellow
At the setting of the sun:
Just an ordinary fellow …
Til the surf was on the run.

And then he rose to glory
As he made his surfboard sing
Through the pipes that play at Manly …
And his board-bird made him king.

But her oldies panned her surfmate
'cause his hair was bleached and long …
They cancelled every surfdate …
Told her that their love was wrong.

Johnny Jacaranda,   Girl sings

---

156. 'Johnny Jacaranda' was submitted as a 'dramatic work' for registration of copyright on 26 September 1967. Registration of copyright was granted on 11 October 1967. Application papers and dramatic work are open for view, NAA, Series number A1336, Control symbol 70014, Item ID. 5021595.

Where are you? Please come soon ...
The clouds are red with blushing
And there is a silver moon,
I see the jacarandas
As they shed their yellow leaves
Like your yellow hair, my Johnny,
And my lonely bosom heaves.

You see her Dad found trouble   Boy speaks ...
Where the surf was rough and high ...
They got Johnny at the double
And he beached Dad high and dry ...
On John's board he caught a wave ...
But the sea took Jacaranda ...
Now the surf's his only grave.

Johnny Jacaranda,   Girl sings.
Johnny, Johnny Jac ...
Thank you Jacaranda ...
You gave my Daddy back;
And I want to tell you Johnny
As the waves begin to sing ...
The purple Jacaranda blooms
Proclaim my Johnny King.

Johnneeeee ...... Johnneeeeeeeeeee .... Jacaran ...... da .

Sound of waves.[157]

____

[157.] Grammar, spelling and spacing are entirely as printed in the documents held at the National Australian Archives.

Index

Index